Wonder AND Wander

An Early Childhood Nature Connection Activity Guide

By Kelly Johnson

With Forward by Dawn Suzette Smith

Wonder and Wander: An Early Childhood Nature Connection Activity Guide
Written and Illustrated by Kelly Johnson
Forward by Dawn Suzette Smith
Published by Wings Worms, and Wonder Neptune Beach, Florida
Printed by Createspace Publishing

ISBN: 978-0-692-12906-7

2018 Wonder and Wander: An Early Childhood Nature Connection Activity Guide by Kelly Johnson is licensed under a Creative Commons Attribution-NonCommercial-ShareAlike 3.0 Unported License.

The information in this book is true and complete to the best of the author's knowledge. All recommendations are made without any guarantee on the part of the author.
The author disclaims any liability in connection with the use of this information.

Access the printable PDF masters from this book:

www.wingswormsandwonder.com/members password: Lampyridae

Acknowledgements

Thank you to all the young children I've known and taught over the years — for sharing their wonder with me, their smiles, their surprise, and their inherent wisdom. And thank you to the adults who trusted me to teach their children, to feed their babies wild berries, to swim them under ocean waves, and to climb them up into trees.

Special love and thanks go to: Sonia & Camillo, Eli & Deo, Emily & Reid, Callum & Caden, Aspen, Kaylin & Spencer, Donavon & Ingrid, Willow & Maggie, Desi & Robin, Zoey, Wells & Adler, Sidney & Manny, Atlas, Keane & Luke, Anthony & Andrea, and the Brighter Day Kids. You are amazing humans and have taught me (and continue to teach me) so much, each in your own unique ways.

This book wouldn't be possible without a little grown-up help too! Huge thanks to: Amy Parmelee, Sara Nail, Lindsey Lowe, Meghan Orman, Julie Williams, Peggy Nolan, Johanna Porter, Dawn Suzette Smith, Kiala Givehand, & Ashley & Rich Diem for your expertise, ideas, and inspiration.

Thanks to the Wintergreen Treehouse, Bay & Bee, Montessori Tides School, the former Discovery Montessori, & DIG Local Network Children's Garden families for the honor of teaching and guiding your little ones.

Special thanks to: Sean, Jeannie, Saray, Maria, Scott, Cathy & Glenn, Carrie, Ryan, Lindsey, Julie, Sunshine, Anna & Mandy, Gary & Dianne, my parents, & my grandmothers for love, patience, role modeling, advice, and unending support of my ideas and adventures!

Join the world of
Wings, Worms, and Wonder!

For more children's gardening & nature journaling books, courses, and inspiration visit...

wingswormsandwonder.com

Access your printable PDF masters from this book +

Bonus Lessons, join the online group, & lots more creative nature connection inspiration, only for Wings, Worms, and Wonder book owners, on the private Garden Party Website page!

Visit: **www.wingswormsandwonder.com/members**

Enter the password: **Lampyridae**

Table of Contents

Forward by Dawn Suzette Smith 7
Preface 9
Introduction 15
Getting Started 25
A Garden Journey 49
Nature Journaling 61

Wonder Activities Introduction 67
Nature Rubbings 68
Play Bouquet 70
Seed Balls 74
Tea Party 78
Nature's Paint Brush 82
Harvest Stamping 84
Rolling Seed Painting 86
Bird Seed Bagels 88
Cloud Watching 90
Ladybug Thumbprints 92
Winter Wonder Clay 94

Wander Activities Introduction 97
Outdoor Color Games 100
Nature Bracelets 106
Ice Catchers 108
Seed Tapes 110
Seed Coats 112
Re-Grow Gardening 115
Sun Color Catchers 118
Leaf Splatter Painting 120
Rainy Day Water Play 124
Garlands 128
Night Nature 132

Closing 136
Resources 137
Children's Herb Primer 142
Works Cited 144

"Nature holds the key to our aesthetic, intellectual, cognitive and even spiritual satisfaction."

~Edward O. Wilson

Forward

"Look, Mom! If you hold them by the wings they can't sting you!" my daughter exclaimed as she came up to me with the wings of a bee pinched between her chubby, little fingers.

While my heart skipped a beat for a moment, I could not help but smile. Little did I know, that was just the beginning of her adventures with insects. One that started with us watching the bees together, in awe of their quick wings and fuzzy bodies, as they buzzed around the large lavender bush in our front yard. I'll never forget that moment and the many others that followed, as I have traveled with my kids on their journey to connect with the natural world.

In the fifteen years I have been a parent and the ten years I have worked helping families connect with nature, I've learned that while young kids are instinctively curious about the natural world, they look toward their grown-ups to help lead the way. They need adults to act as compasses to help steer them in the right direction. They rely on their parents and teachers to keep them tethered to nature when the multitude of exciting toys and gadgets all vie for attention.

Wonder and Wander offers practical tips and encouragement to help parents and caregivers draw young children to the natural world, making nature connection enjoyable and accessible to children and their adults. With gentle reminders like, "Keep reminding yourself that small is perfect in early childhood," Kelly walks parents and educators through the steps needed to create positive nature experiences, quell adult fears, and be role models for children as they develop a connection with the natural world—even if an adult has no experience to draw from.

I've known Kelly for over five years and have only seen her commitment to helping children—and adults—develop a love of nature grow. We have collaborated on projects, shared resources, and I've even taken her inspiring "Draw Yourself Back to Nature Class." Her genuine love of nature and children is matched only by her knowledge of child development, and all of those qualities come together in this practical, indispensable guide.

Wander far and let wonder lead the way!
Dawn Suzette Smith
Co-author of Whatever the Weather

"Live in each season as it passes; breathe the air, drink the drink, taste the fruit and resign yourself to the influence of each.

Be blown by all the winds.

Open all your pores and bathe in all the tides of nature, in all her streams and oceans, at all seasons."

~ Henry David Thoreau

Preface: Seed to Fruit

Often when talking about my family garden workshops, I'm confronted with the question, "But isn't my child too young for a garden workshop?" To which I always reply, "It's never too early to connect children and nature." I discovered, through the many conversations that followed that dialogue, that adults needed a guide for connecting very young children and nature — and so sprouted this book.

From the soil of my first book on middle childhood nature connection (Wings, Worms, and Wonder) grows Wonder and Wander, a guide for helping adults facilitate early childhood creative nature connections. Early childhood, the period from birth to age 6, is an incredibly wonder filled time to spend in nature with children. Everything is brand new and ripe for exploration. As adults gifted with the care of children ages birth to 6, we get to share the child's newness and wonder. To a young child, the simple pleasure of tearing a leaf can bring wide eyes and shrieks of joy, and to me, that wonder is pure magic.

I was immensely lucky to have adults share nature with me as a child, to have jobs immersed in sharing nature's wonders with others, and to be a Montessori teacher for children ages birth to 12.

I entered the children and nature world as a Montessori toddler assistant, spending my mornings in a gorgeous outdoor environment bursting with flowers, fluttering with songbirds and a little freely hopping rabbit hopping, shaded by small trees, and brushed by a fresh ocean breeze. For two years I observed the sense of wonder nature activates in the young child. The magic of those mornings never left me.

Ten years later, when I returned to teaching young children and families in a garden setting, with more nieces and nephews, and more certifications, degrees, and experience under my belt, I fully assimilated the wonder of those previous Montessori mornings spent outdoors with toddlers. The psychological and physiological hows–and–whys of an outdoor environment's allure for the young child now made sense academically. It was also during this second phase working with young children that I began to understand an adult's apprehension to letting young children explore nature. Now in phase three, nearly twenty years beyond that first day in the toddler garden, I am honored to offer adults the means to prepare environments and experiences that spark and sustain young children's wonder.

All while building foundations for unshakeable lifetime bonds with nature. In an ever increasing fast paced digital world, we must create safe natural spaces and activities where children can be free to "wonder and wander" at their own pace.

In her timeless classic, The Sense of Wonder, Rachel Carson declares that,

"…for the child, and for the parent seeking to guide him, it's not half as important to *know* as to *feel*.
It is more important to pave the way for the child to want to know than to put him on a diet of facts he is not ready to assimilate."

This concept of feeling, rather than knowing is, in my experience, key for sharing nature with children. Wonder is a present moment, process oriented, and mindful state. This is the world where the child resides. Knowing, of course, has value in the larger scheme, but in the moment when a butterfly lands on your shoulder, facts about the species can distract us from the wonder of the experience.

There is no need to know the botanical name of a tree to feel peace gazing up into its branches on a summer morning, nor to know the species of a bird to marvel at its graceful swoop through the sky. Those facts retroactively enrich the experience once the moment passes. Save the research for later and relish feeling in the present.

Within this guide, I offer you the tools to gain inspiration and confidence to get outside with young children. Everything you need rests on the following pages. Mother Nature awaits! You can't do it "wrong," and no child is too young (or old), I promise. Turn off the phone, release the constraints of "busy," wander in nature with a child, and let wonder ignite!

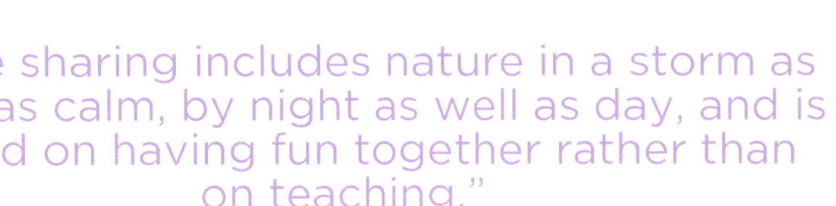

"The sharing includes nature in a storm as well as calm, by night as well as day, and is based on having fun together rather than on teaching."

~Rachel Carson

A Common Language

Clear communication is important. So to ensure that the information in this book is clear to everyone, regardless of their background experience with human development, early childhood education philosophy and methodology, here is a glossary of terms to create a common language and holistic understanding of ideas for the readers. They may also aid in understanding why a child is working or playing in certain ways.

Absorbent Mind - Defined by Montessori as "effortlessly assimilating the sensorial stimuli of the environment…From birth through approximately age 6, the young child experiences a period of intense mental activity that allows her to 'absorb' learning from her environment without conscious effort, naturally and spontaneously." This is the mind's capacity to take in information and sensations from the surrounding culture and environment.*

Sensorial Experience - A term used in Montessori education, particularly in early childhood education. Children are highly receptive to developing the senses between ages two to six and seek experiences that refine their five senses. A sensorial experience allows a child to gather information about their world using multiple senses.

Oral exploration - This is a key developmental stage for learning about the world. Putting objects in the mouth allows young children to sensorially discover the taste and texture of different objects using all their senses as well as prepare the mouth for experiences textures and sensations.

Sensitive period - Specific phases throughout a child's development when they have a predisposition or sensitivity to learning a specific skill. Early childhood is the sensitive period for: order, language, movement, sense refinement, weaning, manners, and culture.

Sensitive Period for Order - Characterized by an inner need for consistency and repetition, the child in this sensitive period craves routines and predictability.

* Learn more about the absorbent mind and sensitive periods at https://carrotsareorange.com/absorbent-mind/

Developmental Plane - Four Stages of physical and psychological growth which are the basis for the age groupings found in Montessori schools. The environment and activities must change as the child's needs evolve as they progress through the planes of development. This book focuses on the birth to 6 years early childhood plane of development.

Executive Function Skills - The skills responsible for concentration and self regulation. These skills are minimally present in birth to 3 years, and developing in ages 3 to 6 years.
- Mental Flexibility - Being able to think about something from more than one angle
- Self Control - Being able to ignore distractions and resist impulsive temptations to accomplish a goal or task
- Working Memory - Being able to hold information in the mind and apply it

Manipulation of Materials - This is the child's act of fully engaging with the objects used for, or included in, an activity.

Order, Coordination, Concentration, Independence - The stages of achievement for the way a child engages wth activities within and moves through a prepared environment toward mastery, whether indoors or out.

Stages of Play
- Solitary Play - Playing alone
- Parallel Play - Two or more children playing near each other but not with each other
- Associative Play - Two or more children playing the same thing, talking with each other, but not working together to create something
- Cooperative Play - Children are working together to play a game or complete a project

Nearby Nature - Familiar nature areas within a child's direct community.

Nature's Whispers - Aspects of nature which are often overlooked due to the daily rush, familiarity, or larger more attention grabbing aspects of the environment. These "whispers" or nature are no less spectacular than grander "shouts" of nature when given close attention and observation.

"If a child is to keep alive his inborn sense of wonder, without any such gift from the fairies, he needs the companionship of at least one adult who can share it, rediscovering with him the joy, excitement and mystery of the world we live in."

~Rachel Carson

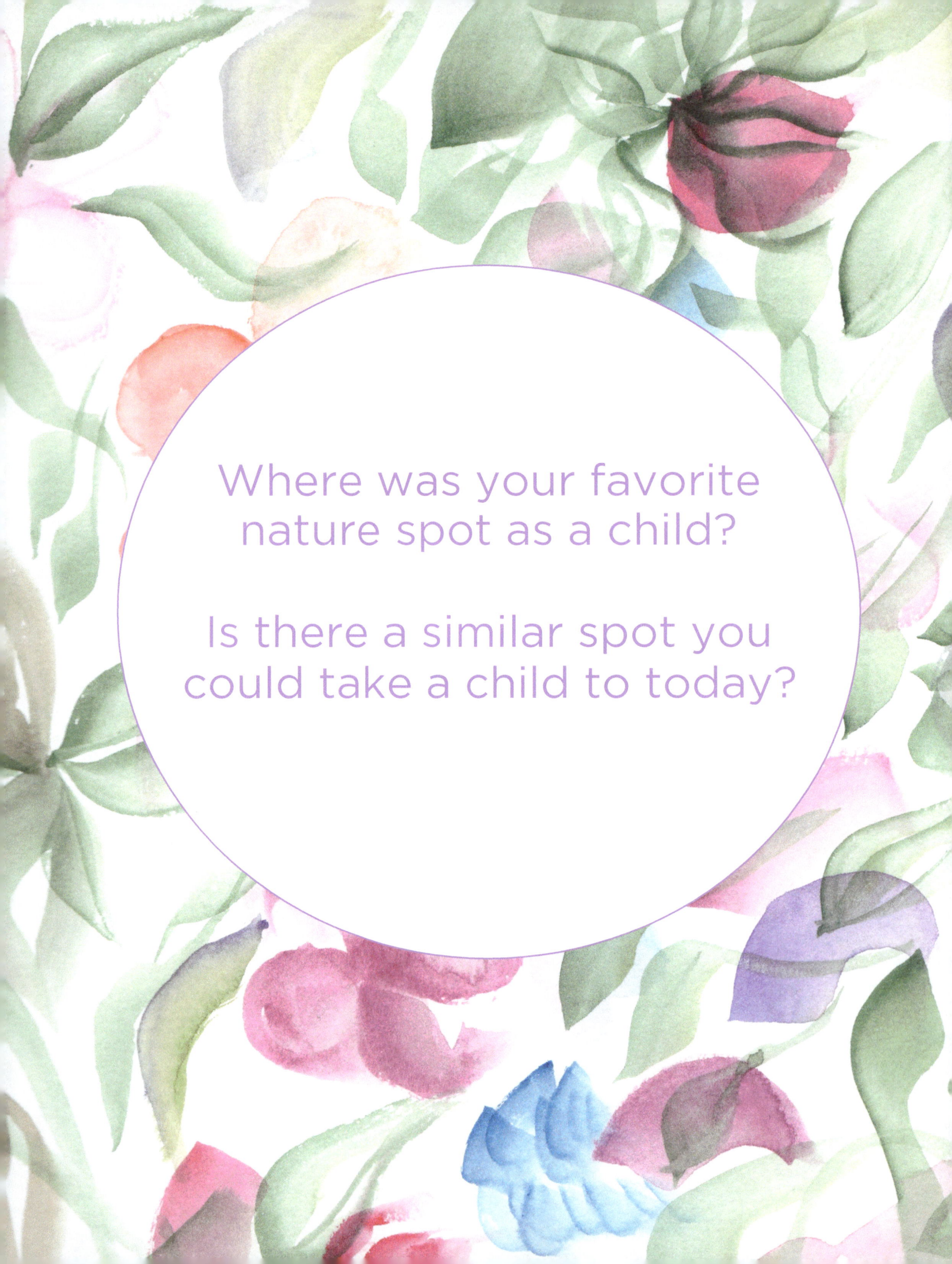

Where was your favorite nature spot as a child?

Is there a similar spot you could take a child to today?

Introduction

Why Connect Young Children with Nature?

Nature connections forged in early childhood provide humans with a base on which grow creativity, peace, resilience, values, knowledge, and even happiness.* Early childhood is the stage when the human mind is developmentally primed for building this foundation. From birth to Age 6, the body and brain are extraordinarily impressionable, receptive, and developmentally seeking to understand the physical world. Our early childhood nature bonds are the bedrock on which we build environmentally friendly lives and conscious communities as adults.

Howard Gardner (of "multiple intelligences" fame) observes that the Eighth Intelligence is the Naturalist Intelligence. The sensitive period for developing this intelligence is early childhood (Checkley). This intelligence could more casually be deemed the "green thumb" intelligence. The perception of having a green thumb may be a learned pattern of thinking that stems to youth, and not a just a genetic gift. All humans are born with a tendency for a "green thumb," or naturalist intelligence. It is an evolutionary survival tool, or as research shows, "…a nature given intellectual culture and ability we all have in order to survive as human beings," (Young 3) according to Gardner's theories. Experiences accumulated in childhood are what define our future relationship with nature and create the idea of green thumbs. This is important because it means that young brains exposed to nature in a regular and positive manner are likely to, unconsciously as adults, view their thumbs as green, and those who experience nature in a negative manner, or not at all, potentially would not. Who knew playing in the backyard at age 3 actually makes us more intelligent?

---

* See more research on the psychological benefits of nature at https://greatergood.berkeley.edu/article/item/how_nature_makes_you_kinder_happier_more_creative . Charles, Cheryl., and Alicia Senauer. "Health Benefits to Children from Contact with the Outdoors & Nature." *Children and Nature Network* (2010). Web.

Get Out There

Getting out there is the essence of wondering and wandering. It is simple enough to say, but it can sometimes be a challenge to actually do. When we prepare a hands-on natural environment in which to let the young child explore, we create the foundations of wonder and connections that children build upon and rely on for their lives. Offering young children bits of wild nature to discover within the safe, structured boundaries of a schoolyard, play space, garden, or backyard fuels their sensitive periods for order, language, and nature — while learning about their world. The child touches, and the brain creates a pathway. The child names, and the nature becomes a part of her vocabulary. When this process happens repeatedly, connections with nature becomes an inherent part of the child's being.

The child age birth to 6 is bursting with wonder for the world. She wants to sensorially experience it all — indoors, outdoors, familiar, and new. As adults, it's the child's unbridled wonder from which we can draw inspiration while guiding the child's journey of constructing a relationship with nature. It's never too late to build a bond with nature and green up those thumbs, so if you are building your naturalist intelligence as an adult, good for you! Cultivating nature connections is all the more fun with a child driving the wonder.

Follow the cues of intuition and feeling, like your child, and learn together. This period of life is a very special time for nurturing natural curiosity and celebrating multi-sensory exploration of every big and little thing in the child's world (Plotkin 88). Like the child, let innocence be the guide, joy be the vehicle, and wonder be the path of this journey into nature connection. "The child is endowed with unknown powers, which can guide us to a radiant future." (Absorbent 4). Let us employ nature to help strengthen the child's desire for a green future world. It can be as simple as a walk outside.

"It follows that at the beginning of his life the individual can accomplish wonders — without effort and quite unconsciously."

~Maria Montessori

Developmental Planes & Expectations

Sparking wonder and building bonds with nature is the ultimate goal of this book — for both young children and their caregivers. Early childhood is a small window of one's life, but the young human changes immensely and more quickly within that window than in any other time of life (paralleled only by adolescence). Cultivating outdoor environments for children ages 0-3 is quite different from that for children ages 3-6. Throughout the book, I offer many ideas to bridge the vast range of early childhood, but it will be up to you, the adult, to adapt or tweak the activities, ideas, and suggestions to fit the needs of your specific environment and children in your care. If a child becomes frustrated with an activity or requires your help, simplify it. If a child is bored or disinterested, add a challenge. And always try again another day. Young children enjoy repetition and sometimes require multiple attempts to spark their interest (like when trying new foods).

In the 0-3 age period, the activities and environment will be explored with the adult close at hand as a guide offering security and confidence. Talk to the young child about what she discovers. Naturally teachable moments for the child to connect with the environment arise often, as do opportunities to develop language. Young children want to explore and learn about their world with, and from, you. When a child and adult are engaged in the same activity with the adult providing the language to describe what the child is observing and experiencing, it's called a "joint attention episode" by developmental psychologists. The 0-3 period is sensorial and primarily explored *with* the adult.

Many adults have a hard time imagining how they can explore nature with a child under 18 months old. To this, I simply reply, "Just take them outside." Hold the infant in your arms, look at the moon, the clouds, up into the branches as the morning sun dapples through, watch the birds, listen to a running stream, feel the wind or a light drizzle, stroll around a garden, and just *be* outside. Touch, explore, lay in the grass, and offer them fruits and veggies to play with as toys. Talk to the child about the world to teach nature language. Tell them the basic names of natural items, explain to them how the weather feels, sit in the shade and let them touch the grass while explaining how soft it feels. Go back to basics and notice how they delight the infant. A little sand may get eaten, clothes may get wet, and sticks may get licked, but the sensorial nature connections derived and the foundations built from these nature–bonding outings will bring immense joy to you both!

> "All that we ourselves are has been made by the child, by the child we were in the first two years of our lives."
>
> ~Maria Montessori

As the child begins to move independently, provide her with safe spaces to test her bare feet on the earth. From 18–months to 3–years-old, the child is ready to engage in more structured hands–on nature activities with their trusted adult close at hand, always ready to offer assistance or security as requested by the child. The child's ability to develop independent mastery of basic daily activities, such as walking while carrying items, picking up small items, and navigating through spaces and objects, skyrockets during this period when given the opportunity. Let nature be the training ground for the 18 month to 3-year-old child to develop fine and gross motor skills. Project–based work is excellent during this time. Remember to always include the language to assist the assimilation of the child's experiences.

Use conversation and the naming of objects and movements as the child completes a cycle of activity.

In the 3-6 period of life, the child becomes much more independent in action and exploration, but also may become anxious as she separates from the close security of the adult. The 18–month to 6 developmental period is when an attraction to the familiar, the repetition of activities, and joy in a small environment will be observed. No nature space is too small or common for the young child. The important aspect is the biodiversity and the ability to touch, move, and work that sparks the interest of the child. By the time the child reaches 5-6 years, provide mentor opportunities for them to teach the younger children how to engage with nature through garden work and outdoor sensory play.

> "From the age of three till six, being able to now to tackle his environment deliberately and consciously, [the child] begins a period of real constructiveness."
>
> ~Maria Montessori

Follow the Child? Really?

When educators advise to *"follow the child,"* they mean follow the child's curiosity, spirit, and sensitive developmental periods, not to let the child be the boss. You are the one guiding an experience created to meet the child's developmental needs and desire for learning about her world. How will the child move through the carefully crafted experience and environment that you create? With focus or reckless abandon? It depends on the external structure and order of the environment. The child's freedom to move through an experience in a constructive way is based on the structure that the experience holds.

Freedom is not to be mistaken with the child being "free" to do whatever they like, such as behaving recklessly or mistreating materials and/or nature. The structure, order, and limits of the environment and experience create the possibility for a type of freedom that allows the child to feel safe and work constructively. This feeling of physical and emotional safety and freedom inspires the confidence with which the child explores and learns in peace and concentration. Montessori method advises that, "We must give the child the freedom, yet be watchful and ready to help." (Lillard 91). Set clear expectations, firm limits, and consistent consequences to create a flowing order and a freedom within the structure of an outdoor environment, learning experience, and even life in general.

THE SCOOP

Life with young children can be unpredictable at best, so be compassionate with yourself as you and the children in your care connect with nature. With every new outdoor adventure, regardless of how it goes, everyone learns something. A "perfect" experience or environment doesn't exist. Some days, a toddler's behavior is just going to be challenging, and that is okay.
They are testing and seeking the limit so they can feel safe knowing where the "edge" of appropriate behavior lies. Keeping structure, in an experience or environment, stems from the space the adult holds. Try your best to stay relaxed, be consistent and gentle in your tone and energy (with the child and yourself), and know however it turns out, you did a great job for the time and place — and there's always tomorrow to try again!

Grow with the Child

As the child grows, so will the environment and activities. If you notice a child becoming bored of an area or activity over a matter of weeks, have them help you add a new plant or feature (think bird feeder and bath or a butterfly puddling station). Also, consider removing activities. If a child repeatedly misuses materials in silly or inappropriate ways, it is an indication that the child is tried, bored, or has lost concentration.

Be alert to this, remove the activity, and engage the child with something else. If discipline is needed, be matter of fact, yet gentle and firm. If a child says, "No!" when presented with an activity, try responding with "Let's do it together." You also can do the activity yourself, and the child often will observe and then join in. If a child shows no interest in a new activity, follow the child's spark of interest for that day and try the original activity again another day.

Consider also, that some activities may just not resonate with a particular child. So if you've tried something three times, and the child still shows no interest, try again in a few months. If they still show no interest, move on. Take things slowly, keep it all very simple, and have fun! If an activity isn't fun for you, the child will pick up on that, so try something new instead.

Adapt and Adjust

Connecting with nature in childhood is all about adapting: the environment, the experiences, and our expectations. As adults, we have lots of expectations. If an experience doesn't meet our expectation, we may feel discouraged. This is our adult tendency for product over process — the exact reverse of the child's drive for process over product. We must let go of our attachments to the product and self-imposed expectations for perfection. Prepare the best you can, and then, like the child, enjoy the process!

The work of guiding wondering and wandering is all about adapting, adjusting, and growing the environment, experiences, and expectations. This includes the expectation of behavior. Certain behaviors are acceptable in one zone of the environment and not in another, just as the behavior expectation of a 2-year-old is very different from that of a 5-year-old. Behavior expectations in a school environment will be more strict than in a home environment, and different still than behaviors expected in a public park or garden. Help the child learn the expectations of when and where a wilder "recess style" movement is appropriate, and when and where control is appropriate. They will likely test these limits, so consistency is key, as is modeling the behaviors you want to see.

These little lessons make big impacts on the development of outdoor learning structure and flow over time. Always be clear about your expectations, as well as consequences, from the beginning. I can't repeat or stress this enough. Limits set by the adult make the child feel safe regardless of how much the toddler may protest in the moment. Feeling safe within the bounds of clear and consistent expectations, limits, and consequences builds the child's confidence to explore, learn, and grow. This clarity meets the birth to 6 child's sensitive period for order while cultivating outdoor learning experiences and environments where respect, wonder, and learning flourish.

Fear

In my years as an educator, I've found it common that an adult's insecurity about her own nature knowledge and experience gives rise to a very real fear to immerse young humans into nature — and a fear of nature in the children themselves.

Is a leaf poison ivy? Does a bug sting or bite? Will the rock they just licked hurt them? An infant is so vulnerable and a toddler so unpredictable when in the wilds of a garden, park, forest, or even backyard — but never fear! Wonder and Wander wisdom is here to ease your mind.

It is important that adults who are around children are aware of how easy it is to inadvertently teach a fear of nature. A simple "Ew, yuck! A bug!" signals to the child that nature is something undesirable. If we, as adults, feel fear toward something in the garden, we could replace "Ew!" with "Oh my, what an unusual creature!"

A positive adult reaction to unfamiliar nature promotes the child's curiosity, desire to learn, and motivates care for nature. Even if fear or repulsion is our immediate internal reactions, reprogram yourself to be curious and open while modeling the same to the child (Young 5).

Remember, the child is looking to the reactions of their trusted adult to know if something in her world is safe.** Save alarm and fear for deserving aspects of nature, such as venomous snakes, so we don't cause undue worry or lose the child's trust by "crying wolf."

** Of course, there are times when safety is an important issue and a firm "NO!" or reaction of alarm is necessary and required. Not everything in nature is safe to touch. Safety is always the first priority, but it is a balance dance of how to express varying degrees of safety or danger to the child.

Teach caution without fear for unfamiliar, yet often harmless, nearby nature. With time and practice, you'll discover that when the unknown or unsettling is approached with caution and wonder, it becomes less alarming and more interesting.

That said, however interesting, there are poison ivy vines, stinging bugs, and items that should not be licked or touched in our natural world. It's a whole lot easier to simply avoid those when experiencing nature with young children. More information on fear and risk assessment is in the next chapter. However, if you are new to nature and don't feel confident (identifying poison ivy for example), I recommend informing yourself on the basics. Start your first nature outings by visiting organized children's nature areas in gardens or arboretums where the facilitators remove dangerous aspects of nature.

They can't control bees or other critters moving through the area, but they will keep the space clear of nests and dangerous plants. Learn from experts how to identify what is potentially harmful; this will help you gain the confidence to independently explore further.

You Are Ready

Think of this guide as not only a how-to, but as your adult security blanket. The aim is to set you on the path for early childhood nature connection success. Of course, there will always be "those days," but fussy infants often calm down when taken outside, and there's no place better than nature for a preschool child with lots of big wiggles. The soothing effect of nature is no coincidence.

Recent research touting the stress-reducing powers of nature is now found in the most mainstream media sources, finally!*** "Biophilia," as Harvard biologist E.O. Wilson coins it, or our genetic evolution to be attracted to natural life, is one reason nature is so soothing to humans (Wilson 1). We enter the world as newborns, day one, with a hardwired desire to be in nature. Start today. Go for a walk with a child, at the child's pace. Winter and summer, rain and shine, let's get the little ones out there!

> "In your child's first four years ... you'll want to encourage and celebrate her natural curiosity and multi-sensory exploration of everything in her world."
>
> ~Bill Plotkin

*** Read the research for yourself! https://www.childrenandnature.org/research-library/results/?h=uDv8hjuZ

Who shared nature with you as a child?

Share your childhood nature stories with a child you know.

Getting Started

Just go outside each day.

Getting started often is the hardest part, so don't let the technicalities of being totally *ready* stop you from heading outside with young humans. A simple walk around the neighborhood has the power to yield just as much wonder as a fully planned, prepped, and executed activity. What this means is that the child is walking (if she can) at a child's pace, and the adults is following the child, stopping when the child wants to touch and explore. It may take 20 minutes to walk one block, or you may not make it past the driveway, and that's okay!

The point is nature connection and discovery, not distance covered. Think process, not product. So while yes, I do stress that preparation is a major key to setting yourself up for early childhood nature connection success, I also encourage you to engage in simple daily nature connection adventures as you prepare more elaborate environments and activities.

Staying Safe and Taking Risks

Safety is of top importance at any age, but particularly so with very young children. Developmentally, they rely on us for their safety, yet alternatively they are in the stage of oral exploration that triggers adult safety alarms nearly 100 times a day. Although some children go through an oral exploration stage more intensely than others, and the length of time varies just as much, there is a point in every human's life where everything goes straight into the mouth.

Sensory input through the mouth is extremely important for child development, and it ranges anywhere from nerve-racking to terrifying for the adults. Real fears, ranging from choking to poisoning, abound. When an adult is uncertain about the nature objects being orally explored, a child constantly putting things in her mouth makes a controlled indoor environment very appealing.

Regardless of being indoors or out, we'll never stop the young human's developmental need for oral exploration. So rather than stay indoors, adults can ease their fears by getting informed.

Here are some first tips:

- Make your yard chemical free. A few weeds and bugs in the grass short term is worth hours of wonder filled play long term.
- Learn some basic backyard plant identification. Check out a field guide, or better yet, seek out a human who can ID local plants and animals, such as a Master Gardener, Master Naturalist, or garden savvy neighbor. They will be happy to go through your yard with you and, at very least, give you the names of plants for further research. I think you'll be pleasantly surprised at how benign average backyard nature really is. This basic knowledge will boost your confidence regarding what plants are safe to be in the mouth, and if any aren't, they can be removed.

Risk Benefit Analysis

Thinking about risk in regard to young children is unnerving, but risk is an important part of life and learning. The analysis of risk benefit is an invaluable life skill. Supervised nature experiences provide the young child opportunities to test developing physical skills and risk analysis with adults close by for reassurance and help. From stepping between garden plants without smashing them and hanging from a low branch, to the bite of a mosquito and skinned knee, with your help the child learns to asses the edge of safety. **Allowing for developmentally appropriate risk is not to be confused with being permissive.** The adult guides the risk, ready to stop the child. By taking appropriate risks, children learn the line between benefit and detriment. They then apply the information gained from experience, analyze its worth and assimilate the experience for later practical application.

THE SCOOP

I'm always getting complimented on my "grass" from people wondering how I keep it green and lush. Well, it's easy! It's all weeds – a.k.a. native plants! I just keep them watered, mowed and edged all nice and tidy and it looks great. Plus, I get the benefit of flocks of robin and ibis who devour any grubs, as well as the beautiful wildflowers that attract interesting pollinators like tiny butterflies.

Risk benefit analysis is an important skill that builds upon itself as the child grows. The lessons learned from risks taken in nature as a young child have shown to be applied to risky social situations in adolescence.* The importance of opportunities for risk assessment, is however, no excuse for lax supervision of the young child in nature. As the adults responsible for the children, we must alway err on the side of caution and care. We must find a balance that works for the adult and the individual child in every environment we encounter. Offer the child room to roam while always staying close enough to quickly remove foreign items from the mouth or prevent a dangerous fall. Set clear limits and consistent consequences ahead of time.

Again, adults must remember to stay calm. Be pragmatic. Ask yourself, "What are this specific child's abilities?"

Then trust the child's abilities. When assessing for yourself the risk of an activity, consider the potential fall or danger — is it fairly small; is it worth the benefit of the child achieving success in the task and building confidence? Before interfering, stand back, observe, let the child work to figure it out, and perhaps offer a simple suggestion for success. (For example if they are having trouble balancing on a log, suggest removing their shoes to see if bare feet make it easier to balance.) Until you can confirm that the activity is not working due to: real danger, child frustration, or the interference of other children, let the child figure it out before you stop them.

Unnecessary alarm and interference distracts the child's concentration and can actually do more harm than good — not to mention deterring their engagement and wonder. When it is determined that the risk is actually too great, panicky alarm doesn't resolve a safety situation more quickly. Safety efficiency comes from staying calm. That said, a firm commanding "STOP!" or "FREEZE!" is exactly the correct and effective safety action in specific cases. Firm direction is more effective than a vaguely instructed command or alarmed shout of what *not* to do.

Trust your instincts, your common sense, & the child's potential.

---

* I can't recommend enough the book *Wild Play: Parenting Adventures in the Great Outdoors* by David Sobel for adults both new to, and familiar with, engaging children in nature from birth through adolescence. Explore an overview of this book on my website blog: https://www.wingswormsandwonder.com/david-sobel-and-the-importance-of-wild-play/ .

As the child progresses through the early childhood plane of development, your supervisory role will change. Obviously, the supervision of a 5-year-old is very different from that of a 1-year-old. As your field knowledge and comfort levels in nature grow, you will gain a solid understanding for how supervision should be conducted and how it should evolve. Additionally, you will learn your children's behavioral tendencies in nature — is she a risk taker or more cautious — and this will dictate your supervisory role as well. As a rule of green thumb, always side with pragmatic caution and seek expert advice when it comes to the natural unknown.

A quick conversation with a 3 to 6-year-old age child about the concrete outcomes of a desired action produces much more successful results than the abstract command of "be careful." Young children may not fully understand *how* to "be careful." Alternatively, offer clear instructions or commands of what the child should actually do or be aware of to stay safe, rather than simply saying abstract commands or what not to do. Conversations that help the child problem solve, become more aware of the environment, and comprehend the outcomes of their physical actions within an environment help the child actually learn how to "be careful."

Alternatives to the basic "Be Careful"

Try these ideas:

- *Observe how...* (the path is unstable, the bank is steep and slippery, there are many people nearby).
- *Notice...* (the poison ivy plants, the baby sprouts near your foot, the big puddle).
- *Move...* (your feet gently, your body slowly, your eyes to the... location you want to go).
- *Do you feel...* (the heat from the fire, coldness in your toes, strong while hanging from that limb)?
- *What's your plan...* (after you jump over that creek, once you're in the tree)?
- *What tools are available to help you...* (dig that hole, catch that beetle)?
- *If you...* (move that log) *where will or what will...* (happen to the creatures living under it)?
- *If you climb...* (on that boulder) *how will you...* (get over it, get down)?

The Environment

A primary concept to remember when curating outdoor spaces for young children is to think small. Montessori writes extensively on the idea of small environments in her book *The Discovery of the Child*, and research shows that young children prefer "direct contact with a small portion of relatively familiar and domesticated creatures and natural settings" (Kahn 132). As adults, we think big, and the young child is expected to adapt to the big world. Our bodies are big and the world generally familiar, but to the small body of a young child, a small space is big with newness. The big world is alluring to the young child, but also it is intimidating. There is an enormous amount of exploration to be accomplished in a flower pot on a patio, let alone an entire backyard.

Urban/suburban families and schools rejoice! You definitely don't need a grand landscaped yard to create meaningful and lasting nature experiences for children. When first planning an outdoor environment, think simple, local, and familiar plants and nature items. Native flora often grows more easily and also attracts wonderful local fauna, such as birds and butterflies.

THE SCOOP

A simple flower pot of grass seed sprouted in a window is a world of sensory wonder for a young child. It sprouts quickly, is very soft, bright in color, smells fresh, and makes a gentle sound when moved. Grow rye or wheat grass to add the option for oral exploration! You can find these seeds in the natural foods stores.

The limitations of the location and size of the environment you are creating (home or school, balcony or backyard, urban or suburban) can actually turn out to be an asset if you get creative. Imagine the outdoor space you create as a nest to nurture the child's sense of wonder and connection. Nature is amazing — let her do the heavy lifting!

The home nature environment and school environment should support each other. For example, parents, communicate with your child's teacher. If they are studying birds at school, prepare bird-themed and bird-watching activities at home. Teachers, send home info on what the children are exploring, storybook suggestions, and a simple activity idea that parents can do to support themes being explored at school. Home and school are two of the most influential environments in a young child's life, and when they align, the bridge further supports the child's development and learning.

Stick to what's nearby and local, set up only a few stations at a time with activities for the child to explore, and think small. Keep reminding yourself that small is perfect for early childhood. Even the most mundane bit of nature to an adult is new and exciting to the child. Be the model of how you want the child to move and interact within the space. Show them exactly how to perform a task. Use fewer words and more clear actions. Remember that parent and child nature experiences will likely be more spontaneous and relaxed than the more structured teacher and student classroom nature experiences.

Location and Zones

When planning your natural environment, think in zones.* These zoned areas will host different activities and meet the child's various developmental interests. Of course, it is likely that you will be working within an established landscape and not looking to totally redesign, so think about the zones you currently have and how they are represented in the areas listed on the following page.

Also consider how zones can be connected and how the child will flow between them. Use curving paths, stepping stones, and even little bridges or very low balance beam style boards. If the environment is in a school or community setting, consider: teacher blind spots, the pockets where groups of children will cluster, and places where bodies may get physically stuck (in the case of toddlers).

Let's Be Realistic

you likely won't have the space for, or interest in, including every zone, so consider other public community nature spaces, such as parks, beaches, forests, gardens, or nature centers for experiences.

* Learn more about zoning early childhood outdoor environments, particularly at schools in Mary S. Rivkin's book *The Great Outdoors: Restoring Children's Right to Play Outside*

Early Childhood Nature Exploration Zones:

- Cultivated areas: flowerbeds, a butterfly garden, or a vegetable patch
- Places to hide and nest: under or within a ring of shrubs
- Climbing areas: a small multi-trunked tree (Crepe myrtle and ligustrum are great for young children to safely climb and hang.)
- An open area for relaxing on a blanket
- An area for water play
- An area for a small work table to snack and work on nature-connection activities
- A wild(er) area

The last zone, the wild(er) area, is the one least desired by adults in suburban yards and most desired by children. This is a zone (however small) where plants grow unkempt, leaves stay where they fall, the wild of nature prevails, and where children find the most joy of all the zones. It's in the wild zone where "don't touch" is checked at the border and the child's imagination drives action (Kahn 45).

The wild zone is the place where the child can do some damage. They can tear leaves, dig holes, break sticks, and yank and stomp on things. For a century, nature advocates have touted that a few squished worms and broken branches in the short-term are small prices to pay for the bonds built between humans and nature in the long-term (Khan 319).

Tearing a leaf is how a child learns about leaves. Yanking a flower helps teach force and gross motor skills. A bit of destruction also teaches the child how to be gentle through natural consequences. Nature is a very special place to be cherished and treated with love, but for a child to become an adult who loves and wants to protect nature, she has to be allowed to experientially learn why nature is so awesome to love. And this is done with a little roughhousing.

Montessori observed that, "When children are placed in natural surroundings, there is a revelation of their strength" (Discovery 94).

Naturally wild(er) spaces provide young children the opportunity to test and evaluate their evolving prowess in developmentally, and behaviorally, appropriate ways.

Curating your existing area as an early childhood outdoor environment (whether home, school or community space) will designate how many zones will be included and their sizes and shapes. Keep in mind that zones can overlap and be multipurpose. For example, a climbing tree could be included in a wild zone, a large flower pot or planter would easily fulfill a cultivated garden zone, and a table easily shares an open space zone. Be creative with your zones and their uses, and, remember, in the end, a little nature goes a long way.

> "For special places
> to work their
> magic on kids,
> they need to be able
> to do some
> clamber and damage."
>
> ~Peter H. Kahn, Jr

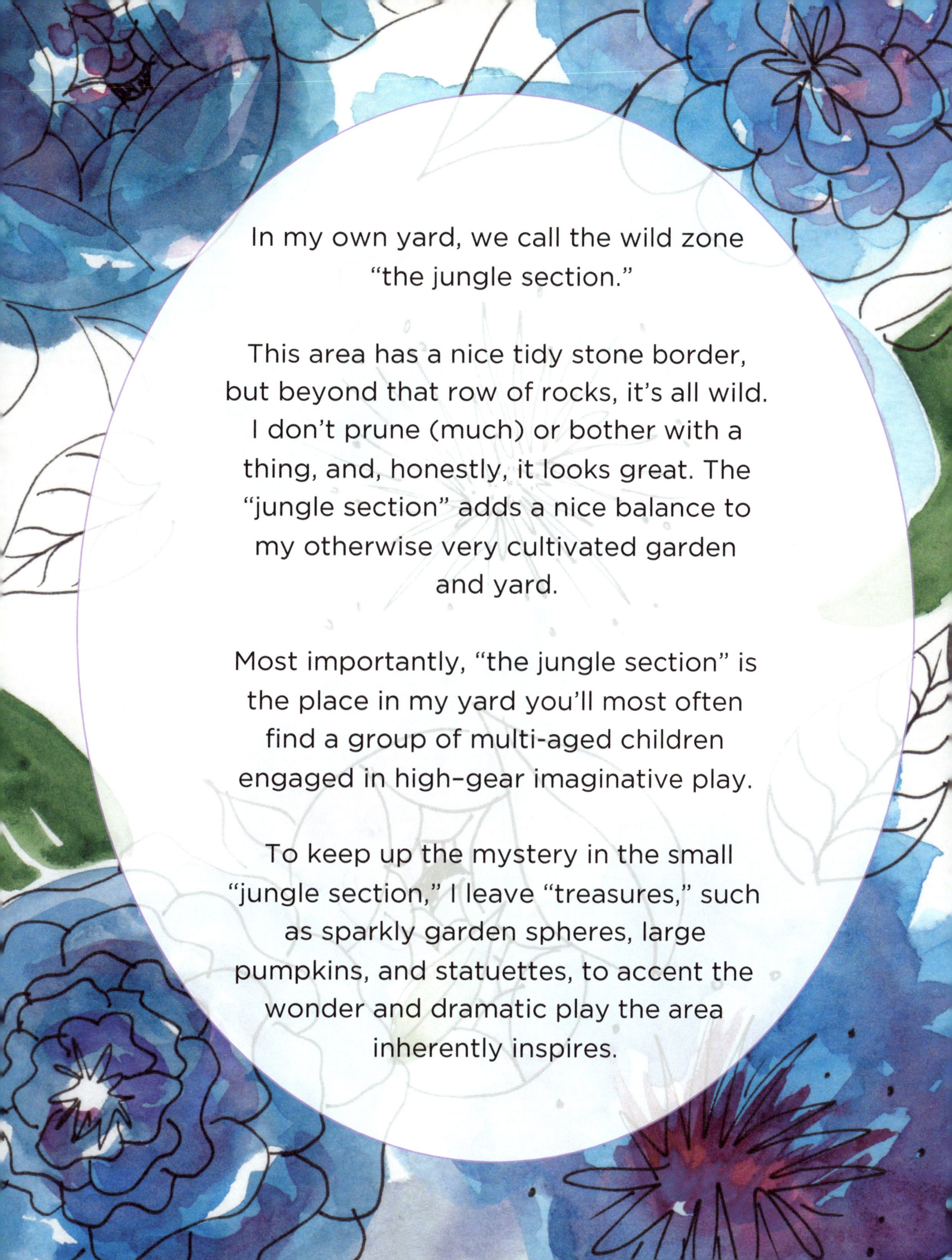

In my own yard, we call the wild zone "the jungle section."

This area has a nice tidy stone border, but beyond that row of rocks, it's all wild. I don't prune (much) or bother with a thing, and, honestly, it looks great. The "jungle section" adds a nice balance to my otherwise very cultivated garden and yard.

Most importantly, "the jungle section" is the place in my yard you'll most often find a group of multi-aged children engaged in high-gear imaginative play.

To keep up the mystery in the small "jungle section," I leave "treasures," such as sparkly garden spheres, large pumpkins, and statuettes, to accent the wonder and dramatic play the area inherently inspires.

Sensorial Stations

A "sensorial station" is what I call a guided or independent spot where a specific nature connection activity is set up for the child. The majority of the activities in this book are designed to be executed at a sensorial station. Depending on the activity and the age of the child, you may be modeling the activity, so consider where you will sit when presenting the activity to the child.

Or in the case of an independent activity, such as a tub of birdseed with scoops, the station can be arranged on a small table for the child to discover and explore independently. Sensorial stations are a fun way to introduce new ways to play, learn, and connect with nature, and they often are the favorite activities that children return to in order to center and sooth their bodies and minds.

THE SCOOP

A sensorial station could be as simple as a cup of water with a bowl of mint leaves that the child tears, places in the water, stirs and drinks (or dumps out) as in the "Tea Party" activity.

Or, it could be much messier such as where the child is presented a bowl of soil, a bowl of water, an empty cup, and a wooden spoon.

I recommend having a change of clothes ready after this one! Regardless of the specifics of a sensorial station, the activity allows for hands-on open-ended sensory play, often done independently. (Some initial adult modeling or encouragement may, or may not, also be helpful.)

Not every foray into the outdoors needs a structured activity by any means. Seemingly "aimless" independent exploration and repetition are extremely important. "Free play" style outdoor activities are linked to stress reduction and the development of creativity and self-esteem (Kahn 55). Sensorial nature play is a basis of the wander part of wonder and wander after all!

When Setting Up a Sensorial Station:

- **Try to use materials that are:** Real, child-size, simple, orderly, and can be used independently of adult help once introduced.
- **Incorporate materials that reflect the child's environment.** This builds familiarity with local nature and place connection. Collect shells on a beach walk or leaves on a hike. Any materials that spark the child's interest are great to incorporate into various sensory activities.

- **Define the space.** Whether on the ground, floor, or table, use a tray or cloth placemat to visually define the work space.
- **Set up activities in sequence order, left to right, top to bottom.** This prepares the child for future reading.
- **Think through each step of the child's process in detail.** Ask yourself, does it flow naturally? If not, tweak the process to work for your space. Remember the child is more interested in the process than the product.

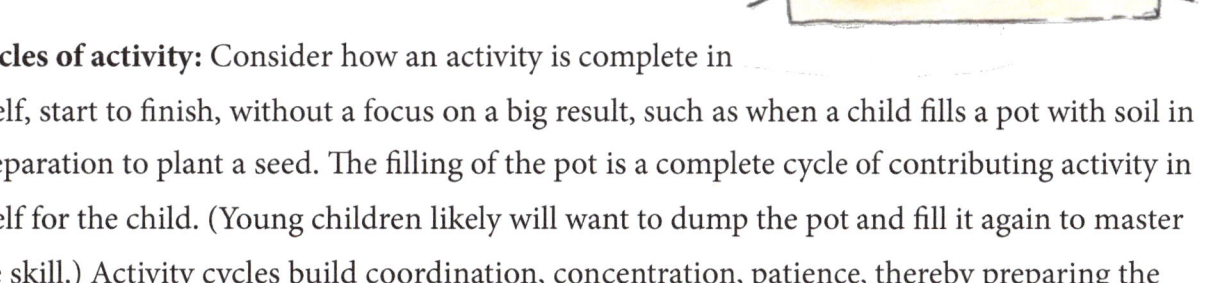

- **Cycles of activity:** Consider how an activity is complete in itself, start to finish, without a focus on a big result, such as when a child fills a pot with soil in preparation to plant a seed. The filling of the pot is a complete cycle of contributing activity in itself for the child. (Young children likely will want to dump the pot and fill it again to master the skill.) Activity cycles build coordination, concentration, patience, thereby preparing the child for the "real life" actions they desire to imitate.
- **Collaboration:** In sensorial and practical work with young children, you provide the structure and order, and the child is the worker, but you may do the work together. For example, let the child participate fully when planting garden starter plants, even if the plants aren't planted quite perfectly. (You can fix them later when the child is engaged in another activity.) This shows the child that they have a role to fulfill in the family (or classroom community), that they have valuable contributions to make, that they are needed, and that they can give to others, while also developing positive self-attitude, and the initiative and confidence that they can "do."

Imitation and Modeling

The young child's greatest desires are to mimic the adults she loves and have a productive role in her environment, just like the adults she observes. If you love to garden, so will she, and if you are afraid of worms, she will be also. The young child is developing the skills to imitate her adults, so we must provide appropriate opportunities for training. Then, she can successfully imitate her adults' actions, and imitate she will!

The value of an adult modeling the nature-based experiences and activities will be very clear when the child works independently. Modeling meets the child's need for imitation training, while exposing the child to nature integrated within daily life.

To best help the child meet this need for imitation, we must model behaviors and actions with mindfulness. Mindful action cultivates focus, quietness, and concentration. Sit quietly with the child while she paints or pets a soft patch of clover. Parallel play with her, or simply sit quietly and observe. Verbalize textures and colors, but not at the expense of breaking the child's concentration.

As adults, we are so uplifted by the young child's joy and capability that it is easy to interrupt their focus with compliments or conversation. We must refrain from interruptions until *we see the child look to us* for help or approval. Only then should we share satisfaction, ask questions or offer further information or instruction.*

Once the child has completed a cycle of concentrated work, share the joy with them! Help them assimilate the experience with language describing the steps, celebrating, and praising them.**

When presenting and modeling an activity, show the child how to do the activity slowly, pausing between steps, with few words. Young children take longer to process verbal steps, so showing is more effective than telling.

---

* If a child is in danger in any way, always interrupt and intervene. Safety first!
** In the classroom environment, praise is addressed in a different way than at home. Unless otherwise noted, in this book I am referring to the parent-child relationship and the at-home style of offering praise and encouragement.

If an activity requires a clean-up step, model that, as well. Then, invite the child to begin the activity. Sit with the child, but let her do the work. Hold back and let the child work in concentration, helping only as needed. If the activity is open-ended and she looks to you for help, ask her what *she* thinks she should do with it, and then offer suggestions after they respond.

Draw awareness to various aspects of the activity through points of interest, like the texture of a leaf, the mixing and sorting of items, or a specific step in the process. This will engage the child in the behaviors you want to see and key details you'd like them to experience in a particular activity.

Remind yourself, once again, that early childhood is a time of amazing wonder, but it also can be emotionally tumultuous. Take it easy and be gentle on yourself and the child. It can be challenging at times when everything is new (to the child and adult).

Even if an activity doesn't go as you hoped or planned the first time, try it again another day. Tweak the process, materials, environment, time of day, and modeled presentation to set up the child and yourself for success. At the very least, you spent time in nature with a wonder-filled little human, and that is worth it all!

THE SCOOP

As hard as it might be, and as adorable as children are when concentrating, try to put the phone/camera away and treasure the present moment. It is distracting to the child in the same way it would be to an adult if someone was documenting our every move.
The present is where wonder and creativity hide, it's where we find connection and joy, and is where the child's mind resides. The memories you gather and bonds you build together with your child in nature's presence will last far longer than a photo posted to social media.

Model **"disconnecting to connect"** for the modern child, a.k.a. putting aside cyber-life connections to connect with life around you. Protect time in the present moment with all your power.
If you want to take a picture, ask the child's permission during a natural break, such as, "Would you like me to take a picture of you with your work?" Then post it later when the child is napping. If the child says no, they don't want their picture taken, respect that.
(This small act aids, models, and teaches consent and boundary respect to be applied in later social situations.) Schedule the space to slow down and disconnect into your daily calendar and watch creative connections grow! There will be plenty other times for photos.

Did you have a special nature hiding spot when you were young?

How could you create special nature hiding spots for the children in your life?

Tools and Materials

The following is a list of some of my favorite tools, materials, and items that help facilitate nature exploration for the young child.* The tools provided will vary, evolve, and grow with the children depending on the environment, season, and ages. Like with the sensorial stations, always opt for a small-size "real" tool rather than toy versions. Real tools set the child up for more success and less frustration.

The list on the following pages is extensive. **You definitely do not need all, or even any, of the things on the list to get started,** but some of these items may be fun, helpful, and interesting to include as you develop your nearby nature environment over time.

- **A Nature Collection Bowl** – A bowl, bag, or basket to transport items indoors ties the indoor and outdoor environments together. You also may want to designate a specific area indoors where this bowl stays, along with, for example, a nature picture book, art supplies, and a magnifying glass that the child can access for further research. (Keep in mind that the child's access to the bowl and the supplies will vary from supervised to independent depending on age.)

- **Basket of Nature Storybooks** – See the Resources chapter for book suggestions.

- **Blanket to relax on and/or small bench**

- **A sandbox** with kitchen tools, buckets, and shovels

"To give children freedom and be watchful and ready to help is not easy, but we must be prepared to do all this."
~Paula Polk Lillard

---

* See the Resource section for tools and supplies referred to in the list and in this book in general. I have received no promotions or compensations to feature any specific products or books. They are simply items that I found worked well for me during my 20 years in formal and non-formal teaching experiences.

- **A Seasonal Sensory Bin or Bowl** – Fill a bowl with seasonal nature items for the child to sensorially explore textures, colors, and materials. This could include:
    - Citrus fruits and peels to smell and taste in citrus season (winter)
    - Sand, clay, and rock salt (and water if you like)
    - Soil and water (mud pie play)
    - Different types of seeds for size, texture, color
    - different seasonal vegetables
    - Leaves of different sizes, shapes, and colors
    - Flowers, ideally organically grown, to deconstruct (a.k.a. tear apart)
    - Any local nature items that are commonly found in your neck of the woods
- **A Nature Journal** – Document in pictures and words your creative nature explorations, discoveries, and connections. See the Nature Journal chapter for more on this topic.
- **Nature Journal Bag** – Or basket to carry the journal, art supplies, field guide, story book, and magnifying glass.
- **Wings, Worms, and Wonder Nature Journal Activity Prompt Cards** – For children ages 4 and up to inspire and guide nature discussion and journaling activities.
- **A Bale of Hay or Straw** – To climb on, jump off, stack if you have more than one, and become any number of pretend objects.
- **A Bag of Play Sand, unopened** – A great walking balancing tool for toddlers. Simply place a bag (or bags) of sand on the ground, unopened. The child will be very entertained stepping on and over the bag/s. If you have more than one bag, place them in a line to practice stepping up and down, and then stack 2 to increase the height as the child masters stepping on one.
- **A Small Stump** – For climbing on and jumping off, using as seat, a place to explore underneath (where roly-polies abound), and when the stump dries children and becomes less heavy, children enjoy rolling them around the yard.
- **Child-size Hand Garden Tools** – Fork and trowel
- **Child-size Stand Up Garden Tools** – metal shovel, rake, hoe, and broom if there is a patio or deck space

- **Child-size Wheelbarrow**
- **Child-size Garden Gloves** – I go back and forth on this as soil contains many microbes that are beneficial for human immunity, but for children who may be afraid of getting their hands dirty, gloves can be used as a transitional tool.
- **Child-size Watering Can** – Choose a style that has a larger hole that is easy to fill from a hose by the adult or submerged by the child into a (supervised) bucket filled with water.
- **A Bucket or Tub of Soil** – The child can independently dig, fill, and dump small flower pots

- **Kitchen Play Items** – Small cups, bowls, plates, tea set, spoons, small pie pans, funnels, sifters, whisks, etc.

- **Glass Jewels and Painted Rocks** – Sparkly ephemera for the child to discover and move around in the space. Choose larger items for very young children to remove choking risks.
- **Bird Feeders, Baths, and Nesting Boxes** – Encourage birds to the yard, or explore and deconstruct found abandoned nests.

- **Butterfly Hatching** – Attract butterflies to the yard with host plants and watch their life-cycles.
- **Butterfly Puddling Station** – A shallow tray of wet sand and stones for butterflies to drink.
- **Rain Gauge**
- **Child-size Easel for stand up art making**
  - **Child-size Water Bucket and 2 to 3-inch Paintbrush**
  - **Small Table and Chair or picnic-style table**

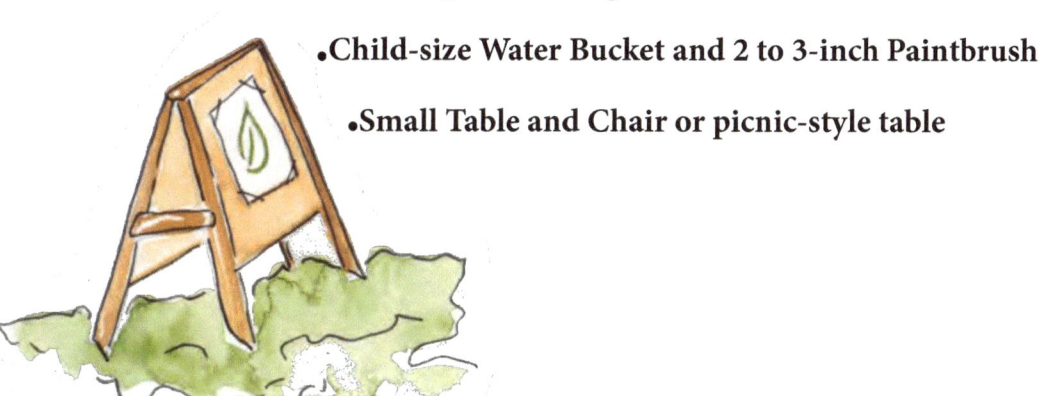

- **Harvest Basket** (and harvest scissors for children ages 4-6)
- **Basket of** – Rocks, pine cones, sea shells, acorns, or other seasonal collected nature items and an additional empty basket to sort and transfer the items.
- **A Bowl or Bin of Bird Seed** – Add scoops, cups, and funnels for sensorial play. Set this activity up in an area where the spilled birdseed is easy to sweep up or can fall to the ground for birds to eat later. (Some seed may even sprout!)
- **Garden Bean Shelling** – In late summer, let the child help you shell the beans from your garden harvest. Or if you don't have a garden of your own, buy some unshelled butter beans or black-eyed peas from a local farmers market and enjoy the shelling process. (This is a favorite activity of my students, and of myself when I was a child.)
- **Muffin Tin or Ice Cube Tray** – Offer natural items to sort into the compartments. Collecting items to sort with the child on a previous day's nature adventure makes this activity even more meaningful. You also can bury the items in, say a bowl of bird seed in summer, box of sand in spring, a tray of wheat grass in fall, or bin snow in winter, and have the child dig the items out and then sort. Some sorting item ideas are:
    - Different types of seashells to sort into each compartment.
    - Two different items, such as acorns and small pebbles, and the child fills one side of the tin with pebbles and the other side with acorns.
    - Water and land items, such as seeds and seashells, to observe the differences and sort accordingly.
    - Toy animals and other seasonal small toys like eggs or pumpkins.
    - Once the child masters sorting, let the child practice pouring. Put the sorting tin on a tray, and have the child pour water into the sections using a tiny pitcher. Have a clean new sponge available for the child to clean up pouring spills and then squeeze the water back out into the pitcher
- **Loose Parts** – This is the term used to describe providing an assortment of natural objects that the child manipulates freely. Loose parts could be as small as natural blocks made from tree limbs to actual limbs for 5-and 6-year-olds to use to build a simple fort.

- **Two Bowls and a Set of Tongs** – Move nature items between bowls using the tongs. Add water to the bowls and explore how items sink or float.
- **Colander, child safe chopper and cutting board** – For preparing fruit and veggie snacks to share in the garden. The children especially love to both harvest and prepare a garden snack. Herbs, strawberries, string beans, peas, carrots, broccoli, cherry tomatoes, edible flowers, and even radishes are seasonal harvest favorites for little hands.
- **Wet and Dry Play** – a.k.a. Mud pie play. Children can create mud pies and then observe (and engage with) how mud changes when it dries.
- **Watercolor Paints and Brushes** – To paint in the nature journals, on the easel, and even on snow in winter play.

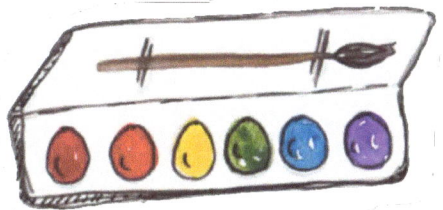

- **Sidewalk Chalk**
- **Outdoor Music Play Supplies** – Pots and pans to bang on, wind chimes to clang, and kazoos to toot; anything that makes noise can be an outdoor instrument.
- **Play Clay** – A classic favorite whether store bought or homemade. (Find recipes in the Wonder section's "Winter Wonder Play Clay" activity.) Offer cookie cutters as well as fresh picked herbs and nature items to mix in with the clay.

"Personal experiences carried out on reality form real knowledge."

~Maria Montessori

Begin With Foundational Experiences

There are many simple foundational and grounding activities and experiences you can cultivate to bring the children closer to nature in a concentrated and heart-centered way while helping them acclimate and relax into an outdoor environment. These activities also help the child aged 3-6 to distinguish the differences in outdoor time between free play and nature lessons.

- **Sensory Observation** – This is an activity that is great to do with humans of all ages, and I open my nature journaling and school group workshops with this activity. It really grounds the children (and adults) in the environment by allowing physical and mental quietness to make space for tuning into nature. This is a simplified early childhood version of the full sensory observation lesson in my book Wings, Worms, and Wonder.

Try this:
- Invite the child to take three deep breaths.
- Then, go through each sense, inviting the child to bring their awareness to the senses by having them touch the sense corresponding body part gently (sight/eye, smell/nose, hearing/ear, and touch/skin). Noticing aspects of the environment in the present moment with each sense. Curate this activity based on the attention span of the child/children. With children ages 0-2 years, standing or sitting, hold the child in a peaceful natural setting. Do the observation yourself while verbalizing your observations and actions to the child. With children ages 2-3 years, choose a single sense to focus on at a time and encourage them to verbalize their observations. With children ages 4-5 years, guide them through the senses, reminding them to wait to verbalize their observations until the end.

- **Singing** – Humans have been uniting together in sound while engaging in a group activity even before speech.* To help the child ground into the nature environment and prepare the mind for connection, sit together and sing a simple nature-inspired song. This sets an intention while signaling to the child this is a time to be outside and focused, rather than simply running around.

- **Storytelling** – Like singing, storytelling is at the essence of humanity.** Reading and telling stories about nature helps children learn about their environment and builds their confidence in nature. It's never too early to begin reading to children, so why not read outside? Read seasonally appropriate and environmentally significant fiction and nonfiction books in the garden to spark wonder and learning. Also, provide a small basket of a few durable nature books for the child to independently browse or choose for you to read.

In addition to reading, children 18 months-6 years can use stories (and songs) with actions to learn about many cycles and creatures in nature. Embody the natural world: Pretend to be worms wiggling through the garden; a sprout emerging; a caterpillar changing into a chrysalis and butterfly; or do some plant and animal yoga poses.

THE SCOOP

I start my children's garden workshops with a modified secular version of the storybook song Inch By Inch.

Children look forward to this part of the workshop as it clearly defines the starting point for them. Once we sing, they know it's time to control their bodies, listen, and engage with the activity.

* Learn more about humans and singing - https://www2.lawrence.edu/fast/KOOPMAJO/antiquity.html

** Learn more about humans and storytelling- https://www.pbs.org/wgbh/pages/frontline/shows/religion/story/oral.html

- **Walking on the Line** – This is a classic Montessori 3-6 childhood activity that can be easily re-created in nature with many fun variations.* It helps the child develop control of movement. You can seek out natural lines in nature, such as following paths through trees or following animal tracks, or you can create your own line that weaves through a garden space using a long string, ribbon, or line of sticks.

    If you are making the line, you may want to arrange it in a circle to allow for continuous flow. Then, invite the children to stand on the line (or beside it and, perhaps, barefoot if seasonally appropriate). Model carefully walking heel to toe on the line at a steady pace. You may want to sing a simple song or chant while you walk. Explain that while you are singing, they will walk, and when you stop, they will stop.

    Then, invite the children to walk following the line, keeping a somewhat equal distance from each other. This will help them develop balance and concentrated mind-body movement awareness. To add challenge to this activity, children can carry found objects, such as rocks or pinecones in their hands, or use one hand to hold an object on top of their head for a real challenge.

The Wonder and Wander Activities

The birth to 6 developmental plane encompasses a huge spectrum of abilities and skills. The instructions for the activities in this book are generally targeted at the 3-to 5-year-old child. Specifics for younger children are noted otherwise within the lessons. Additionally, I offer ideas and suggestions to simplify for younger children or increase the challenge for older children where applicable. Teachers and parents should find the lessons easily adaptable to the needs of their particular children and environments. They are a jumping off point for hours of outdoor fun!

Preparing for the Wonder and Wander chapter activities in this book is just like preparing for a sensorial station. The following activity preparation ideas are tips to get you going with the activities. Some of the tips will sound familiar, but they are good reminders and are worth repeating. Preparation is a key of success!

---

* Learn more about the Walking on the Line activity at http://www.infomontessori.com/practical-life/control-of-movement-walking-on-the-line.htm

Activity Preparation Ideas

- **Choose materials** that are real, child-size, simple, orderly, and that can be used with minimal adult intervention, and eventually, independently, once modeled.
- **Before presenting a new activity to the child**, think through each step of the process in detail, and if you are unclear, even practice it yourself. Remember, the child is much more interested in the process over the product.
- **Be realistic regarding children's attention spans.** They are short and can even be as short as one minute per year of their age. Remember, just because a child engages with an activity for only four minutes at first, they are likely to return to it within the same nature play session, so keep it available. Break components of the activities up over a couple days to keep them short. (For example, collect leaves on a walk one day, tear them up the second day, and make a garland the third day.) Then, as the children grow in age and attention, activities can include more steps within a single period of time.

- **Set up activities in sequence order** left to right and top to bottom within a defined space. For example, set your activity materials upon a tray or placemat on the ground, on a blanket, or on a table. Then, model the process slowly, pausing between steps, then hold back and let the child work in concentration, helping only as needed or when asked.
- **Draw an awareness to points of interest to engage the child** in the topic or behavior you would like to see or explore. For example, use phrases such as, "Oh, I see an acorn! Let's pick it up" or "Look! We can scoop this soil into this bowl. Would you like to try?" This type of language clarifies the challenge of an activity, engages a child deeper in the process, and draws them back to the work if concentration is lost.

Let's Begin!

Remember, at the end of the day, it's simply about getting outside and learning more about our natural world. However simple, however messy, or however crazy, any time spent outside is a good time.

I stress, you *do not* need to collect all the tools and materials, create every sensorial station or extension for every lesson, or prepare perfect zones to begin enjoying nature with young children and using this book.

Regardless of your stage in the preparation process or familiarity with nature yourself, go ahead, get out outside with your little ones. Be gentle with yourself, push judgement and comparison aside. Children and nature don't judge, so neither should you. Relax and in the present space of where both you and the children are at the moment - physically and developmentally. Congratulate yourself for taking steps to connect chidlren and nature. Then, keep getting out there. Start simple today and grow as you go. It's good for them, for you, and for the Earth!

"It takes a whole village just to raise one child, don't say they actin' wild if you ain't walked that mile, in the shoes of the innocent youth."

~Dat Bu, from the song "Village"

A Garden Journey

Gardening with Young Children

A garden where a child safely explores nature on a small scale is a huge asset to wondering and wandering. This garden could be in a backyard, schoolyard, community garden, botanical garden, or park. There are a few key elements that make a garden perfect for early childhood, such as freedom of safe picking; child friendly plants; specific varieties of plants chosen for sensory exploration; and developmentally appropriate opportunities for garden maintenance work. Remember that no natural area is too small for the young child; it's all about quality of space, rather than quantity.

Assimilation and internalization of the garden is also important for planting seeds of Naturalist Intelligence in the young child. Reading is a great way to aid this, with the added bonus of increased language development. This section offers information, tips, ideas, and activities for creating a small garden space potentially accessible to the child on a daily basis in all seasons, as well as ideas for using nature-based literature in conjunction with natural garden spaces, designs, and planting plans.

What you plant in your garden, and when, will vary greatly depending on where you live. For help, check the Resources section in the back of the book for finding your climate zone for planting; contacting local Master Gardeners and County Extension Agents for beginner gardening help; get the Wings, Worms, and Wonder Let's Build A Garden plans for building, planting and maintaining your own raised-bed garden; and for Wings, Worms, and Wonder children's garden consultations.

Familiarize yourself with all the nature opportunities offered in your community, such as community garden children's workshops; botanical gardens; nature trails; nature centers; family friendly small farms; arboretums; public parks; and nature preserves. Many are free (or offer free specific days and times), and provide a vast variety of learning opportunities with experts and volunteers in various environments, from prairies and woodlands to seasides, riverbeds, and beyond. Most of all, and most importantly, visit natural spaces regularly with the child to wonder and wander, at their pace.

What veggies would you most like to grow in a garden?

Do any fruits or vegetables have a sentimental value for you?

Start with those!

Garden Building Basics

Materials

- Pots or garden beds
- Soil
- Plants and seeds
- Access to water

Preparation

- Decide what type of space you have for your garden. Will you choose a very large flower pot on a sunny patio or porch, or will you plant a garden bed in the yard?
- Explore your climate zone and learn what veggies you will plant according to where you live and the season. This is a key step in setting your garden up for success.
- Relax and let go of any preconceived notions that your thumb is not green. It's okay. The child doesn't judge and is learning just like you. Celebrate the fact that you get to approach the garden with the same beginner's mind as the child. What fun!
- In each stage of the process, involve children of all ages in developmentally appropriate ways.
- Explain to the child that you will be planting a garden together. Walk around the space with the child talking about what seeds and plants need to grow (soil, sun, rain, and love). Ask the child if she thinks the spot is sunny enough, will get rain or access to water, and would she like to help care for the plants. Then, explore the answers with them based on the features and limitations of the space in which you will grow your garden.
- Read stories about gardens (see the Resources section for ideas) and draw pictures of gardens in a nature journal (more in the next chapter on nature journaling with young children).

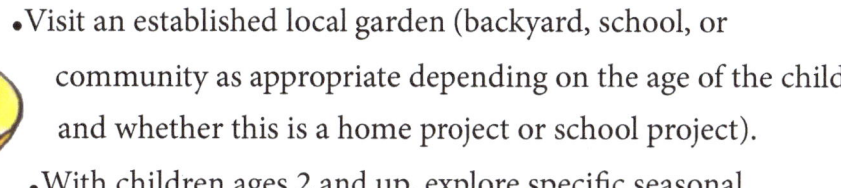

- Visit an established local garden (backyard, school, or community as appropriate depending on the age of the child and whether this is a home project or school project).
- With children ages 2 and up, explore specific seasonal vegetables that could be planted in your new garden. Taste them, touch them, look at the fruits and the seeds, and have the children participate in deciding what veggies to plant.

Building a Garden

- Choose what type of small garden suits your environment and lifestyle.
- Collect the items and supplies and then set-up, build, or arrange is appropriate.
- Choose building tasks that are safe for the child to participate in. Obviously this will depend greatly on the age and capabilities of each individual child involved.
- Children ages 3-6 are helpful with most jobs, excluding using power tools and carrying very heavy items, of course. Children age 2 and older can use a hammer safely when taught how to do so. Children ages 18 months and up (who are walking and standing independently) can help dig with child–size shovels and transport soil using child–size wheel barrows. Infants enjoy observing the process when cradled by a loved one outside and being allowed to touch the plants and the soil. Be sure to chat to the infant about the project the family is working on together, naming (and holding when appropriate) the plants and tools, and explaining the jobs to include the child in the process and develop nature language.

Planting

- Choose a selection of both seeds and "starts" (the small veggie plants bought at a garden center or farmers market). You don't need to grow a huge selection of plants and seeds. Choose just a few, so as not to overwhelm the child (or yourself), remembering less is more when it comes to young children.
- I recommend growing the following plants directly from seeds: peas, beans, squash, cucumbers, pumpkins, corn, carrots, beets, radishes, okra, and sunflowers.
- For best success, grow from starter plants: greens, tomatoes, herbs, broccoli, lettuces, cabbage, edible flowers, and strawberries. These plants take much longer to sprout and can sometimes be tricky for beginners to get established. The easy path is hard enough, so set yourself up for success!

THE SCOOP

Find lots of gardening tips and tricks on the Wings, Worms, and Wonder website — from container gardening to when to harvest to natural bug sprays and much more!

- Before planting, explore each of the seeds and plants, observing their colors, sizes and textures. Talk about the basic parts of a plant: roots, stem, leaves, flower, fruit, seed. It is great at this point to also show examples of the fruits the seed or plant will produce.
- When planting seeds, show the children how to make a little hole with their pointer finger and place one seed in each hole. I like to pose the question, "Can you grow if I sit on top of you? No, that is silly! We all need space to grow. That is why we only put one seed in each hole. Just like you, plants and seeds can't grow when they are squished either."
- When planting starter plants or "starts," show children how to dig a hole for the plants slightly bigger than the root ball gently remove the young plant from the container, place the young plant in the hole, and cover up the rootball with soil. (I like to say, "Be gentle with the little plant just like you would with a baby, because this is a baby plant.") Help the children bring intention to the planting act by having them send the plant into the garden with a good wish, such as "Grow big little plant."

- Water the newly planted garden, giving each new plant and seed some water. Keep the new garden watered until the seeds have sprouted and plants are established. This will be approximately two weeks, depending on the time of year, soil temperature, soil composition, and rainfall. Then, cut back the watering to every other day, or as needed to keep the soil moist, but not soggy. You don't want the garden to dry out. If the garden is in a container it will likely need more water than an in-ground or raised-bed garden.
- Once the seeds have sprouted, add a light layer of hay or mulch to conserve moisture.

Maintain Your Garden

- Once the big work is complete, spend time enjoying your garden! Try to get out to check on it at least four days a week.
- Notice how the seeds and plants are growing and changing. Look for insects. (Children are great at this.) Check soil moisture, remove weeds, and simply enjoy the wonder of how a garden grows. Young children enjoy the process-oriented work of garden maintenance very much. They receive the physical and psychological benefits of nature connection in the process, as well as the benefits of repeat activity progressing toward mastery of tasks.

> "Why try to explain miracles to your kids when you can just plant them a garden?"
>
> ~Robert Brault

Harvest and Sharing the Bounty

Harvest time is the favorite time! Harvest day is the portion of the process children (and adults) most excitedly await. To be able to grow, pick, and eat a veggie, all yourself, is a small miracle of life and produces immense wonder. It is also wondrous to parents how children who previously refused veggies on their plate will excitedly eat veggies they pick themselves. I've seen this in my own work innumerable times.

- Include the children in harvesting! This is the most exciting part — and better yet, they like to eat what they harvest. Offer them each a harvest basket or bowl to choose their own harvests. Teach them how to properly harvest without damaging or pulling out the plant. ("Pinch or cut, rather than yank and pull.") With very young children, plants will get yanked out, but it's okay. They can always be replanted and the child's harvesting joy is more important. Show them how to pick more gently next time and avoid reprimanding them for accidentally yanking out the plant because their motor skills aren't fully developed.

- Involve children in the final stage of the garden process — cooking. Young children love to cook when given the opportunity. Watching an 18-month-old child prepare a snack and serve it to her friends is a wonder many adults hardly believe possible until seen with their own eyes. Young children are fully capable of chopping veggies with safe tools (see Resources), tossing salads, helping to prepare a homemade salad dressing, and even serving bowls to their fellow diners. It may take a little longer and require a bit more clean up, but the short- and long-term rewards of completing the garden cycle with the child are well worth the extra time.
- What are those rewards? The child will eat (or at least willingly and curiously taste) the food she prepares. She will take pride in serving her harvest to her friends and family. She will foster a loving connection with nature through home-grown food, the creative process of cooking, and confidence stemming from community contribution. Together, these add up to healthy food relationships.

All in all, gardening is a process filled with wonder, surprises, excitement, and, honestly, for even the most experienced gardeners, some frustration. Birds may eat your berries, aphids may eat your beans, and fungus may decimate your squash, but that's all in a day's gardening and happens to the best of the bunch. As you gain experience, you'll learn how to spot an army worm before it devours your tomato plant, learn when to give your squash calcium before too many fruits are lost to blossom end rot, and know when to harvest your cucumbers before the borers get too deep into them. It sounds crazy, but it's all part of the gardening journey! Embrace the wild adventure of the garden through the eyes of your child, remembering process over product. You'll both be rewarded in wonderful ways by Mother nature.

> The work which pleases children most is not so much that of sowing seeds as that of harvesting... It is harvesting; one might say, which intensifies the interest in seed sowing"
>
> ~Maria Montessori

Life Lessons & Literacy Within the Frame of Gardening

Read! It's as simple as that. From day 1, read your infant books. Read them stories, poetry, fiction and nonfiction, and about everything you love in nature. Infancy is a great time to read adult gardening books. Read them aloud so the child benefits while you gather knowledge. Read indoors and read outdoors. Reading to a child is a great way for you to gather knowledge that you can apply down the road, while bonding with and helping with language and reading development in the child.*

Once the child is about 6-9 months, teach her to turn the pages and point out objects in the book. Starting at 9 months, always have books available within the child's reach. When they are 5-6 years, schedule both an aloud and a silent reading time into the daily schedule, where you also read. Although the child may not actually be reading silently yet, they are independently looking at the pictures, naming, and forming stories in their head (or aloud to themselves).

> "One of the greatest gifts adults can give — to their offspring and to their society — is to read to children"
> ~Carl Sagan

Frog & Toad teach good things come to those who wait

Classic children's book favorites such as Frog and Toad, by Arnold Lobel, teach lessons through the nature lens on slowing down, patience, and keeping our peace. In the Frog and Toad story "The Garden" from the book of short stories *Frog and Toad Together*, Toad learns a lesson in patience when he tries to grow a flower garden as beautiful as Frog's. This story is a wonderful reminder that when we keep our peace and patience, it benefits us, as well as all everything and everyone around us.

Learn more about supporting literacy in early childhood https://www.naeyc.org/our-work/families/read-together-support-early-literacy

Frog and Toad Activity

- Read *The Garden* and discuss the story together.
- Plant sunflower seeds in a flower pot. Use raw, shelled, unsalted, seeds. You can get these in the sprouting section of a natural foods store. If you soak the seeds overnight before planting they will sprout more quickly. Spread a layer of seeds covering the soil's surface, then sprinkle a light layer of soil overtop.
- Then, a day or two later, before the seeds have sprouted leaves, dramatically role play that you are very impatient that the seeds are growing so slowly.
- Ask the children how they feel about the seeds taking so long to sprout. Read the story *The Garden* again. Over the period of time between reading and when the seeds sprout, observe and care for the seeds, while engaging in the philosophy of patience through the eyes of Frog and Toad.
- As the children ponder the idea of patience and waiting, while waiting for the seeds to sprout (a virtual eternity for a young child), use the opportunity to discuss ways that patience is beneficial in life. For example, in the garden, harvesting slowly prevents plants from getting damaged or yanked out of the ground, while walking with controlled feet through the garden rows, house, or classroom prevents tripping or stepping on things.
- Ask children ages 3-6 ways they use care and patience in the garden and their wider lives and have them draw slowly to calm music. At appropriate moments, engage even younger children in conversation ideas about waiting. It's never too early to model a dialogue of ideas.
- In their nature journals, have children ages 5-6 years draw themselves (and perhaps even Frog and Toad) being patient waiting for seeds to sprout, and share their drawings. You may want to write their dictated thoughts about their patience picture in the journal. (And remember to do the same and share yourself.)
- Draw the sprouts in the nature journal once they sprout. Then, when the sprouts are about 2 inches high, snip them with scissors, like you are giving them a haircut removing their leaves and about an inch down the stem. Wash well and have a delicious healthy snack!

Beatrix Potter's "Tales" model behavior outcomes

Beatrix Potter's Tales series is a timeless resource for teaching children about life through nature. These books are a personal favorite of mine. Although her animal characters do wear clothing and speak, they are always illustrated correctly, they exhibit behaviors specific to the actual animals, and all the plants, gardens, and habitats portrayed in the illustrations are realistic, seasonally appropriate, and planted correctly. Beatrix Potter spent uncountable hours throughout her childhood and adult life observing and drawing plants and animals. Her deep understanding of natural history gives her illustrated stories a realism unparalleled in other anthropomorphized children's literature.

Additionally, Potter led a socially isolated childhood, which resulted in her exploring various human social relationships through the actions of the animals in her stories, such as Tom Kitten's disaster in dress clothes, Squirrel Nutkin's lesson on negative attention seeking, or Peter Rabbit's debacle in Mr. MacGregor's garden. Each story gives children a cause-and-effect example of behaviors the child may want to test, and what may happen if they do, while also entertaining and teaching about nature.

Potter's "Tales" Activities

- Read *The Tale of Peter Rabbit* and plant a version of garden like Mr. MacGregor's garden based off the illustrations. Choose a couple plants that he grew and plant them just like in the story's illustrations (perhaps Peter's favorites: lettuce, radish, and french beans).
- Like the illustration in the book, plant beans in the back on a trellis, with lettuce next, and radish up front. This is in a height descending order so all the plants get enough sun.
- Remember keep it small. A few seeds of each variety is just fine.

- If you're feeling ambitious, or are a seasoned gardener, plant cabbage, onions, parsley, and chamomile also. Carrots can also be planted in between the beans and lettuce for fun.
- Then, draw the garden as it grows in all seasons in the nature journal, just like Beatrix Potter.

- On a rainy day, read *The Tale of Mr. Jeremy Fisher*, go out in boots and splash in puddles.
- On a clear day, visit a marsh, pond, creek, or river, and explore the plants and animals found along the edges of fresh water. Watch for birds and waterfowl, feel the slimy wet underside of a water lily pad and the soft dry fluff of a bulrush flower (a.k.a. cattail), look for turtles, minnows, and, perhaps, tadpoles if the season is right, and listen for frogs and toads.
- In autumn, read *The Tale of Squirrel Nutkin* and go outside to explore the chatter play and busy nut–collecting work of squirrels. Then, outdoor role play squirrels having the children collect and bury acorns or other nuts local to your area.
- With children ages 5-6, read the book *Beatrix Potter and Her Paint Box* by David McPhail to learn more about Beatrix Potter's life as a girl and her nature journaling.

"Set the children free, let them have fair play, let them run out when it is raining, take off their shoes when they find pools of water, and when the grass of the meadows is damp with dew let them run about with bare feet and trample on it;

let them rest quietly when the tree invites them to sleep in its shade;

let them shout and laugh when the sun wakes them up in the morning, as it wakes up every other living creature which divides its day between waking and sleeping."

~Maria Montessori

Nature Journaling

Journaling with Young Children

Each time we venture into nature, big or small, we are impacted, but when we can assimilate those experiences through images and words, we form deep bonds. We understand the natural world, and our roles within it, more fully. As adults, when we understand our ecological relationships, we can help children do the same. Plus, your nature journal is also a great place to document the wonder you see through your child's eyes and the awe–inspiring accomplishments they make while discovering their natural world.

I have found that nature journaling, using both pictures and words, is an incredible way to embrace ourselves as part of the amazing web of life. Nature journaling opens up creative flow. It makes us slow down and become quiet observers. It gives us a place to assimilate our experiences and to ask questions for later answers. It allows us to embrace our genetic heritage as a species evolved from, and continually supported by, the Earth's beauty and bounty. It clears the way for our senses of wonder to bloom. It's never too early to develop a journaling practice for the family or class. Start drawing and writing with the children about nature experiences big and small, near and far.

From a weed busting up through the sidewalk to a vacation at Yosemite, observe and explore, and let journaling bring a fullness to your everyday nature experiences.

Nature journaling and nature art are excellent ways to help children (and all humans) assimilate their nature explorations. Very young children can sensorially explore textures, smells, and tastes through nature art with material manipulation. Creating collages, cooking, and herbal projects are just a few such ways. Within the journal of a young child, they draw and paint their experiences and discoveries, however representational or abstract. They are encouraged and guided through this process by their trusted adult. Once the art is complete, the adult can then chat with the child about their experience and even write the child's dictation to the page. (Ask for permission before writing on the child's paper, unless it is clear before they start that you will write their thoughts on the drawing, especially in the case of 3-6–year–old children.) Using pictures, and then words, helps the child assimilate the nature experience while building a base nature vocabulary and a visual history. If nothing else, early childhood drawings and observations are both adorable and insightful!

Journaling one's nature observation and experience through creative expression fosters a reliable process for children that encourages the assimilation of how the outer natural world is part of their internal life dialogue. Using nature journaling in tandem with story, song, sensorial activities, collection bowls, nature shelves, and independent indoor and outdoor hands-on exploration concretely connects young children and nature. In addition to the child using a journal to assimilate experience, nature journaling by the adult along with the child encourages, models, and validates the process, as well as displays an appreciation of nature, art, beauty, and wonder for nature.

Be sure to have some fun with your own nature journal and share your discoveries and drawings with the children. (Never shame your own drawings in front of the child, or in general. Children don't judge. They will love everything you make, I promise!) You will be pleasantly surprised at how your own relationship with nature deepens, thanks to the child's wonder and a nature journal practice. Furthermore, in school environments, nature journaling aids teachers and guides in anecdotal assessments of the children's connection strides and the effectiveness of an outdoor program or lesson.

THE SCOOP

If given an entire blank book, young children often like to fill all the pages in one sitting. In lieu of this, provide the young child with loose pages of the same-sized paper, then bind them into a journal, folder, or binder. This is a practical way to create seasonal or yearly journals in a fairly consecutive way, and it will save you on blank notebooks.

Is my child too young to journal?

When is the time to begin journaling with young children? As soon as a child shows an interest in mark making, it is time to begin a nature journal practice.

Provide the 18-month to 3-year-old child with a journal book or paper, and no more than two colors of crayons or paint at a single time. Children ages 4-6 may request more colors. For children younger than age 3, let them make marks as they please. For children older than age 3, show them leaf rubbing and tracing techniques, as well as beginning drawing with basic leaf and flower shapes. Casually point out the actual shapes and lines in the object they are drawing.

Unless specifically asked for help by a 4- to 6-year-old, never correct unrealistic aspects of their drawings. Be sure to keep drawing experience loose, and let the child lead the way when it comes to their expression of the object. Additionally, any structured drawing time should not replace opportunities for free drawing.

Once the child is finished with a journal entry, rather than offer basic compliments of "That's so good!" engage the child in meaningful open-ended conversation about her art.

Using conversational language in conjunction with nature journaling opens the child to talk about the nature observations and experiences she is creating and assimilating. Additionally, refrain from making assumptions about the child's drawing, as what the child intended may not actually be what you see in the drawing. For example, if a well meaning adult says, "What a cool flower!" The drawing could actually be a frog. Placing incorrect assumptions and labels on a creative expression could close the child off to future nature art connecting and journaling. This is more applicable to children ages 5-6, but it is good to keep in mind anyway. Instead, employ the questions and conversation starters above and become pleasantly surprised at the depth of thought put into the art by the child.

~ Willow, age 5

Try These Phrases:
As additions or alternatives to traditional praise, and to open up creative conversation with children about their nature journaling and art.

- *I see you worked very hard...* (on this area). ***Could you tell me more about it?***
- *What part do you like best?*
- *Tell me about what you created* (drew, painted...).
- *What inspired you to choose those...* (colors, lines, shapes, textures)***?***
- *I noticed you really concentrated on this...* (green) ***area.***
- *I can see you carefully observed the....* (green of the leaf, line of the branch...).
- *What do you think about your...* (drawing, journaling, observation)***?***
- *Did you find any part of this work to be challenging?*

- Ask the 4–to 6–year-old child if she would like to add labels to the journal entry — for example, the name of the leaf or its parts.
- Offer children who are interested in writing if they would prefer to trace or copt letters that you write. Labeling engages the child in written nature vocabulary, as well as further conversation about the documentation of their observations.

Nature journal regularly, in various nature locations, and keep it relaxed and fun. Nature journaling is a wonder-filled way to connect with nature that is steeped in historic legacy. Natural historians from John James Audubon, to George Washington Carver, to Rachel Carson all kept nature journals, so you are joining good company!

Nature journaling unites our analytical observations with our emotional connections by balancing head and heart in a nature-inspired creative process. Start children journaling early, journal as a family or class, schedule journal times each week to integrate it into everyday life, and the children will inherit a place in the legacy of nature journaling naturalists. Moreover, they will have a tool for life to help process their relationships with the world.

"It begins with a knowledge of his surroundings. How does the child assimilate his environment?...The child absorbs these impressions not with his mind but with his life itself"

~Maria Montessori

Create a Nature Journal Art Basket!

All you need is:

A designated basket or tote bag
Paper and Journals
Pencils and Erasers
Color pencils
Crayons
Tape
Glue stick
Watercolor paint
Paint brushes
A Small cup for water
Napkins
A magnifying glass
A ruler

Wonder

Our Sense of Wonder

Our human sense of wonder is the magic of which childhood, and life, is made. It's the root of our curiosity, creativity, and drive to learn. Our big beautiful natural world is so chock full of wonder it can feel almost overwhelming at times. That is why tapping into wonder with the young child is so wonderful. It allows us to think small and appreciate the little everyday bits of natural wonder.

We don't need a big pristine national park to evoke sense of wonder (although big wild nature is wonderful and important too, don't get me wrong, but that's a different conversation). To hear nature's whispers, pay attention to the little often overlooked familiar bits of natural wonder around us everyday. Like a child, we need only a single flower and an open mind to find wonder in the familiar.

In This Section

You'll find activities that will evoke wonder using the arts and creativity. Many of these activities can be paired with the nature journal, although not always at the same time depending on the age and attention span of the child. They each invoke observation and connection by encouraging listening to nature's whispers with all the senses.

Let imagination and creativity be your guides in these activities. Use the activities as jumping off points for further exploration and make each your own. The children will burst with many ideas on how to expand on various aspects of each lesson, so roll with that. Follow the child's flow, offer warm smiles of encouragement, do the activities *with* the child, while being sensitive for cues when to step back and allow the child to work independently. Remember, if the child becomes silly or disengaged, redirect them to a new activity and try again later. Above all, have fun!

Nature Rubbings

Leaf rubbings are an easily overlooked activity because they are so common to us. To the child, however, a rubbing activity is like a magic trick — something appears from nothing!

Make rubbings in your nature journals of anything and everything flat you find. With your assistance, rubbings teach the young child about colors and textures while developing fine motor skills. To the older child, rubbings can teach basic anatomy of a leaf and provide a creative process for making patterns and designs inspired by nature.

Materials
- Large crayons with the paper removed (Crayons with flat sides are especially great.)
- Paper – loose or in a journal
- Flat(ish) Nature Items - such as leaves, flowers, and bark
- A hard surface like a clipboard, tray, or surface/table

Preparation
- Place a few flat nature items on a tray or in a bowl.
- Place a piece of paper or a journal on a tray with a crayon or two in seasonally appropriate or matching colors.

Procedure
- Invite the child to the table or blanket with the natural items and the rubbing materials.
- Explore the natural items. Name and sensorially observe their textures and colors.
- Model for the child how to place the nature under the paper, and then cover it up with the paper.
- Model how to hold the paper down with one hand, and the crayon by its side. Begin to rub the paper. Express wonder when the rubbing begins to appear.
- Explore the rubbing when it's complete. Look at the leaf under the paper and back at the rubbing, comparing.

- Invite the child to try. Hold the paper for them at first and help them regulate the pressure needed to make the rubbing to set them up for success until they get the hang of the process. Younger children may want to watch you make multiple rubbings (perhaps even on multiple days) before trying themselves.
- Model how to hold the paper down with one hand, and the crayon by its side. Begin to rub the paper. Express wonder when the rubbing begins to appear.
- Explore the rubbing when it's complete. Look at the leaf under the paper and back at the rubbing, comparing.
- Invite the child to try. Hold the paper for them at first and help them regulate the pressure needed to make the rubbing to set them up for success until they get the hang of the process. Younger children may want to watch you make multiple rubbings (perhaps even on multiple days) before trying themselves.

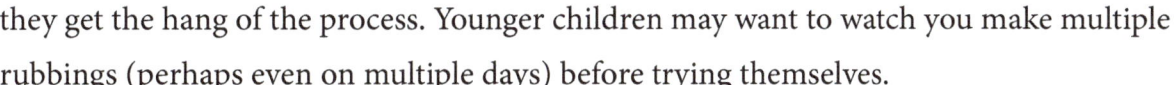

Extensions

- Once the child masters the rubbing process, she can make rubbings from trees, rocks and other parts of nature to which they bring the paper to, rather than place under the paper at a table.
- Children can label the anatomy of the item from which the rubbing was made, or add the name of the plant and where they found it.
- Use rubbings made on loose paper to make cards to send to friends and family, and cut and glue collages from the rubbings.

Play with a Bouquet

In all seasons, flowers bring cheer indoors and out, but usually we get to enjoy them only with our eyes and maybe our noses. In this activity, the children get to collect and deconstruct the flowers and enjoy the beauty of each of the flower's parts individually. This activity is great for children starting at about age 1. The primary difference is what flowers to use. Generally, up to age 3, use edible flowers, as the child may want to orally explore the parts of the flowers.

Edible flowers can be found at specialty grocery stores and often at farmers markets. Pansies, violas, and day lilies are common edible flowers that are easily grown in a backyard garden or flower pot. I recommend growing edible flowers for fun anyway because older children enjoy eating and adorning their harvest feasts with flowers, too! The main thing to keep in mind with this activity, is to let the children fully sensorially explore pulling apart the flowers. Nature journaling, card matching, and labeling doesn't need to happen the first (tenth, or ever) time this activity is presented. It is primarily an extension for homeschoolers and older children. Follow the child's interest and let the questions they ask be a clue as to when is the right time to present the journaling and labeling.

Materials
- Flowers –
    - Store or farmer market bought flower bouquets (Buy organic to prevent contact with the poison sprays used in conventional growing.)
    - Harvested from a nature walk (always being mindful of protected wild flowers and flowers that may be poisonous),
    - Home or garden grown.
- 2 bowls
- Tray
- Nature journal with pencils, color pencils, or crayons

- **Optional for 4 to 6-year-old children:** scissors, flower part labeling cards copied from this activity, flower name labels of the particular flowers being used, a basket or small tray for the cards and labels.

Preparation

- If possible, take a walk with the child and collect flowers from the garden. This should be done on a day preceding the actual activity.
- If not, take the child to choose a ready made bouquet from a local farmer or store, organic if possible. A local florist or farmer may even give you older flowers they can't sell for this activity if you develop a relationship with them.
- Place the flower/s to be explored in a bowl, if using small or edible flowers, or on a tray, if using bouquet flowers with longer stem.
- Arrange an empty bowl for flower parts to be discarded to the right of the flower bowl or tray.
- Optional: Discover the names of the flowers you are using in the bouquet. If using name labels and/or flower part cards, print them out and place them in a small basket.

Procedure

- Invite the child to the table or mat where the flowers are presented.
- Offer the names of the flowers if that information hasn't yet flowed into the conversation naturally.
- Show them how to pull off the petals, leaves, break the stem, and say the names of the parts.
- Explore the different parts, noticing the shapes, colors, textures, and any particular features and differences in the particular flowers. This may include counting the number of petals and the number of leaves; looking how a petal's color fades between two or more colors; exploring the stamen and pistil (children ages 3-6); and noticing the differences in markings on various petals. (For example, on a pansy, the lower petals have dark markings that guide the eye toward the center of the flower, or more specifically, the eyes of the bees needing to pollinate the flower, compared to how the upper petals are without these markings.)
- Have fun with the basic wonder of the sensorial exploration of pulling apart flowers, investigating, and considering all the parts and their uses. Tear the parts of the flowers to see the insides and explore the textures.

- Provide the flower parts cards (see next page) and see if the 3-6 age child would like to match the parts of the flower she has deconstructed to the corresponding cards.
- Offer the nature journal and drawing materials to the child to draw the parts of the flowers in the nature journal. (The drawings may be fairly abstract depending on the age of the child.) Offer the name labels to children who are exploring writing to label their flower parts drawings.

Extensions

- Play with bouquets in various seasons using many different types of flowers. Getting locally grown flowers from farmers is a great way to learn what flowers grow in what seasons in your area. You could even visit a farm and learn how to plant your own cutting garden.
- Add a flower arranging twist. Offer the child a small vase and a few flowers and sprigs of greenery with stems. Show them how to make a flower arrangement in the vase. Toddler-age children may have an interest in placing flowers in the vase and then moving the flowers or vase to new locations to practice walking while balancing the vase. Children ages 3-4 can be offered a small pitcher of water to fill the vase. Offer a sponge to clean up any spills if the child is participating in the water-pouring work. Children ages 5-6 can create increasingly larger arrangements for daily enjoyment or festive celebrations. As the arranged flowers die back, play with deconstructing them.

- Dyed flowers. This is great fun when daisies are in season and can be picked by the child on a walk, but can be bought as well and any longer stem white flower should work. Place water and food coloring of your choice into a cup. Cut the bottom inch off the flower, and place it in the colored water. Within an hour or so, you will notice that the petals start changing colors!

    If you want to get really clever, split the stem vertically about 3/4 of the way up, and put half the stem in one colored water cup and the other half in a different color.

    The flower will turn the two colors! This is great to do before lunch or nap, as the color doesn't change instantaneously, then when the child returns later, the flowers will have changed colors like magic!

    Older children can draw the flowers and the color change in their journals, and even make a color chart exploring which colors work best and why this works. (This activity also illustrates exactly how the plant draws water up the stem to its petals through capillaries, just like the child draws water up a straw).

THE SCOOP

Get a printable pdf of the Wings, Worms, and Wonder Parts of a Flower card material from the "Garden Party" webpage.
Find the log-in information on page 4!

A trick to helping cut flowers stay fresh longer in an arrangement is to cut about an inch off the bottom of the stems before placing them in the vase with water. This fresh cut increases the flower's ability to uptake water.

Seed Balls

Seed balls are great sensorial work. Choosing the right seeds for the right place is key for the seed balls to successfully sprout. Also, consider the areas where you want to spread them, how much water those areas get, the time of year you will be spreading, and variables like foot traffic and public mowing. Or, if you feel your thumb is less than green, choose your seeds based on they shape and texture of the seed, and use this as a purely sensorial activity and leave the sprouting success rates up to nature.

Seed balls can be made in two methods, soil and paper, soil messier than the paper, and both styles are included below. Try both styles because they each provide equally fun but different sensorial experiences. There's a high chance that ages 0-2 children may try to eat the mix, so consider your particular child/children's tendencies for oral exploration and plan accordingly. I recommend using the paper seed balls with ages 0-2 and both paper and soil seed balls with ages 3-6.

General Materials
- Seeds – Young children quite enjoy picking apart marigold and sunflower seed heads and this activity can be explored a week prior to making the seed balls.
- A tub for mixing the base and seeds together
- Drying rack of some sort – Cookie cooling rack, screen rack, tray

Additional Materials for Soil-Based Seed Balls
- Self-hardening clay: This can be bought at a craft store (terra-cotta or gray, not the brightly colored waxy modeling clay) or, if you are in an area with a lot of local clay, dig it up from the ground for free!
- Potting soil, organic with no added fertilizers or chemicals, as young children will be handling it.

Additional Materials for Paper-Based Seed Balls

- Paper – Approximately 1 inch wide strips of newspaper, newsprint, or regular shredded paper. The amount of paper you use will depend on the amount of seed balls you want to make. Two daily newspapers make about 20 seed balls. Non-coated papers work best, so throw out the ad pages if using newspaper.
- A strong blender or food processor — if possible, use an old pitcher because the newspaper ink can be tricky to clean off.
- Warm water
- Optional: turmeric or beet powder to add color
- Muffin tins or cookie cutters to shape your seed balls a bit more fancy

Preparation

Before beginning, research appropriate native wildflower varieties for your climate zone to help choose what type of seeds you would like to spread. Great options for North America are: cosmos, milkweed, coreopsis, coneflower, sunflower, and marigold.

Making seed balls is not an exact science and gets messy, but that is okay and all part of the fun! Let the children mix and mash together the materials and enjoy the natural textures of combining the ingredients.

THE SCOOP

Allow time for sensorial exploration of both the soil and clay mix and the paper pulp. The children get really involved with kneading these mixes and enjoy it immensely.

Remember to keep it relaxed. Both of these "recipes" will likely require adjustments depending on your ingredients.

Soil-Based Seed Balls Procedure

- Get a hunk of clay the size of a handful. The handful size depends on the size of the hands. Children will use smaller hunks of clay, and adults larger, as fit their hand.
- Flatten the clay into a pancake, about 1/4 inch or so thick (This is a basic guideline, not an exact science.)
- Firmly press a handful of potting soil into the top of the clay pancake. A general ratio is 5 parts clay to 1 part soil to 1 part seeds (again, not an exact science).
- Knead the clay and soil together. You want the seed balls to stick together, rather than be crumbly.
- Sprinkle a mixture of the seeds you chose onto the clay pancake. The seed balls can be a single-seed variety or a combination.
- Press the seeds into the surface so they do not fall off when the clay pancake is picked up.
- Fold the clay, soil, and seed pancake in half and then in half again.
- Knead the clay, soil, and seeds together so they are fairly well-blended.
- Roll the mixture into a ball.
- Pull off chunks from the bigger ball and roll into smaller gumball size seed balls.
- Place all the seed balls on a tray to dry for a few days.

Paper-Based Seed Balls Procedure

- Soak your shredded paper in warm water for about 30 minutes to loosen the fibers of the paper, making sure the paper is submerged in the water.
- Once the shredded paper is soaked, add 1/2 cup of water, blend it to a pulp in a powerful blender or a food processor. If you only have a regular blender, blend your paper in small batches. Add more water if needed to blend easily.
- If you are adding anything optional or extra colors using natural powders, do it at this stage while the pulp is still a little watery.

- Squeeze out any excess water from the pulp.
- Give each child a tray or bowl with the pulp.
- Show them how to sprinkle the seeds into the pulp and knead to combine.
- Shape the seedy pulp into balls or press into a muffin tin or cookie cutter molds.
- Set your seed balls, or seed shapes, onto a drying rack to dry.

Spread Your Seed Balls
- Once dry, spread your seed balls!
- Give the seed balls as gifts, toss them into flower pots, out into the yard, or on the town!
- For the best long-term results, spread the seed balls in areas that are not mowed regularly. Don't be shy, spread lots of them! You're a wondering and wandering guerrilla gardener!

Extensions
- Read books on bees, butterflies, and the other wildlife that will be attracted to the seeds spread in the seed balls.
- Plant a couple of seed balls in pots so the children will be able to identify the sprouts and plants coming from the seeds they spread.
- If you spread the seed balls in the yard or community, after a couple months, retrace your route and see if you can find any that have sprouted. (It can take longer in the "wild" because of environmental factors, such as rainfall.)
- Make extra seed balls and have the children decorate paper bags. Package the seed balls in the bags, and sell them at a school or community fundraiser.
- Draw the different seeds used in the seed balls in a nature journal to practice observing the seeds.

Tea Party

Herbs are a wonderful way to introduce young children to the smell and taste senses in the garden, and what better way than with a tea party? Depending on the age and dexterity of the child, tea can be made in two ways. Ages 18-months to 3 will place the herbs directly into a jar or pot of water, while ages 3-6 will fill actual tea bags and make custom tea blends. Since the presentation of this activity is different for the two age ranges, the instructions are separated below. This activity also can be done with dried herbs if fresh are unavailable. See the Resources section for a Children's Herb Primer with great suggestions for sensory rich child friendly herbs!

Materials

- Fresh herbs picked from the garden, or store bought. Good choices are: basil, fennel, roselle, lavender, chamomile, sage, lemon balm, and stevia.
- Drinking cups
- Hot or warm water
- Fillable tea bags (see Resources)
- Stir sticks
- A mason style jar, quart size, glass or clear plastic - When children are taught to move with concentration and awareness, glass is safe for a young child and is used widely in Montessori toddler classrooms.
- Mesh strainer
- Paper or reusable straws
- Optional: Edible flowers and a natural sweetener, such as honey or agave (There are different recommendations on when young children should eat honey due to it containing a spore bacterium called *Clostridium botulinum*, which in rare cases can cause infant botulism, so to be safe, never give children honey before age 1 at the earliest, as generally advised.)

Preparation

- Help the child harvest and wash fresh herbs, or sort dried herbs, and sensorially explore them.

Tea Party Procedure Ages 0-3

- Offer the child a small-mouth mason-style jar filled half way with water. Yes, these are glass so the very young child should not walk around with the jar; it should be left on the ground or table. Older children who have practiced moving while holding glass should still leave the jar stationary and bring the herbs to the jar, rather than jar to the herbs.
  - Show the child how to tear apart herb leaves and edible flowers, and place them into the jar.
  - Model smelling the different herbs, and engage a conversation describing the different smells.
  - Allow the child to explore tearing and placing the herbs, offering the child a straw or stir stick to stir the mixture.
  - When the child is finished adding herbs to the water, allow them to use the straw to drink their "tea" from the jar, or strain the water into a cup and have a tea party!
- I personally don't use sweetener, beyond stevia herb leaf, with this age group.

Tea Party Procedure Ages 3-6

- Offer each child a fillable tea bag
- Model how to tear apart the herb leaves and edible flowers, and then place them into the tea bag.
- Model smelling the different herbs and engage a conversation describing the different smells.
- Allow the child to independently explore tearing and placing the herbs, and encourage the child to stuff the tea bags fairly full. This will create a more robust tea once steeped.
- When the child is finished adding herbs to the fillable tea bag, close the tea bag, as per package instructions, and place in a heat-proof cup.
- Add hot or warm water to the cup, and let the tea steep 5-10 minutes. If using a sweetener, add while steeping.
- Offer the child a straw or stir stick to stir their tea.
- Add an ice cube if the tea is too hot to drink (or if children are too eager to wait).
- Enjoy a tea party out in nature!

Extensions

- Talk about observations made from the leaves and flowers of the different herbs used in the tea. Then, with 4-6-year-old children, draw the plants in the nature journal.
- Press various herb leaves in a heavy book, and then glue them into a nature journal.
- Sun and Moon Tea. Gather mint leaves and water in a clear glass jar. Steep it in the sun for 6 hours to make sun tea. Or steep the mint tea overnight in moonlight under a full moon.

THE SCOOP

Tea Party Twist: Bath Time Tea Bags

Materials

- Herbs - harvested by the child or store-bought
- Readymade drawstring nut milk strainer bags (see Resources), or light cotton muslin fabric to sew your own pouch, and yarn or ribbon to tie the pouch. If sewing your own, I recommend making a simple 6-inch x 3-inch pouch sewn on three sides.

Bath Tub Tea Procedure

- Give each child a pouch and have them stuff it about ¾ full of any herbs they like from either the garden, previously harvested, dried, or store bought herbs (fresh or dried).
- Tie off the top with a piece of yarn or ribbon, or if using a drawstring readymade bag, just cinch it up.
- Optional: Add a couple of drops of chamomile or lavender essential oil before cinching to give the bath tea bag an extra olfactory boost.
- After the bags are filled, store them in the fridge until bath time to keep the herbs fresh.
- At bath time, place the tea bag under the faucet to steep while the tub fills. It can be left in the bath with the child as well, but that may result in leaves in the bath (which isn't so bad).
- After bath time, discard the herbs from the pouch, and hang the pouch to dry to refill another day.
- Optional - Adventurous bathers can add herbs and flowers directly into the tub and fill to take their "tea" bath with the herbal "loose parts."

Nature's Paint Brushes

Whether using fingers, brushes, or stamps, painting is a time-tested favorite activity of children. When they are offered unique bits of nature to use as an alternative painting tool, it adds more fun! Create nature's paintbrushes ahead of time and then offer them to the child to paint in the garden — or en plein air (a.k.a. outdoors) as the Impressionist painters called it.

This activity is best done with children 3 years and up.

Materials
- A few thin sticks, approximately 4-6 inches long and about a finger size, 1 inch diameter
- Any brushy type of natural items that can be attached to the stick to make a brush, including green leaves, green pine needle or fir bunches, grasses, and flowers
- Yarn, string, twine, or twist ties to attach the nature items to the stick
- Paper
- Paint - Tempera paint is great to use with young children. Offer the child only two or three coordinating colors.
- Cups or bowls for the paint

Preparation
- Gather the natural items into bunches with the thinner ends together.
- Bunch them with the stick, so they are about an inch up one end of the stick (like making a tiny broom).
- Wrap the string or twist ties around the bunch and the stick, so the nature items hold securely.
- Decide if you will have an easel for painting on large paper or paint on smaller paper at a table.

Procedure

- Model to the child how to dip the brush into the paint and apply paint to paper.
- Show the child how to mix colors or keep designated brushed for each color (although brushes may not stay designated).
- Allow the child to paint, and paint along if the child is proficient at using the paint with less supervision.
- Enjoy the inspiration that nature brings as you both paint away!

Extensions

- Use leaves, pebbles, bark, and other found objects to dip into paint and stamp onto the paper.
- In winter, use nature's brushes with evergreen needles and liquid watercolor paint to paint on the snow.
- Look at children's books about Impressionist painters and get inspired to paint outside regularly.
- Build your own outdoor easel for regular plein air art making. (See Resources)

Harvest Stamping

In this activity we take garden to table literally by using veggies to decorate a placemat! A cloth placemat is a lovely way to designate a work or eating space. Make garden-inspired placemats for holidays, gifts, or as a way to add connection to the origins of the veggies on the plate. I like to do this activity in late fall when the root veggie harvests are plentiful.

Materials

- Cloth placemats, approximately 8 x 10 inches. You can make your own from cotton fabric cut to size and then stitched around the edge to prevent fraying, or buy cotton placemats. Wash the fabric or placemat before stamping to remove any sizing or starch.
- Acrylic paint — choose two to three colors of paint that coordinate when mixed. ** scoop (Avoid complimentary colors, red/green, blue/orange, yellow/purple, as these will turn muddy when mixed.) Great color combinations are green/yellow/blue, orange/red/yellow, pink/purple/blue, red/violet/fuchsia. White can be added with any of colors, as can metallics such as gold and silver.**
- Seasonal fruits and vegetables, perhaps even harvested by the children from their own garden. Carrots, apples, potatoes, broccoli, cauliflower, and peppers cut vertically work well, or any other not-very-juicy produce.
- Plastic plates or aluminum trays for paint
- Water, rags, protective table cloths or paper, and any other cleanup materials needed for non-washable paint in your environment
- Optional: smocks, clothesline and pins or drying rack for the stamped placemats, and permanent markers to add the child's name and date.

Preparation

- Prepare a placemat for each child.
- Protect any table surfaces, if needed.
- Cut the fruits and veggies to be stamped. Cut carrots, apples and potatoes in half horizontally; cut broccoli, cauliflower, and peppers in half vertically to get "tree" and trefoil shapes; or use any other not-very-juicy produce local to your area. Three veggie varieties is an ample selection.

- Place the fruits and veggies to be stamped in a tray or on a plate.
- Place paint onto the plates like a palette.

***Acrylic paint does not wash out of clothes. Because it won't wash out is why it works so well for placemats. Plan accordingly with smocks, old clothes, or let the children create au natural. Acrylic paint in non-toxic and easily washes off skin.

Procedure

- Gather the children, away from the fruit and veggie stamping table, and show them the different fruits and veggies available to them on the table. Name them, observe their beauty, and engage the children with stories about how they grow.
- Explain that they will use these particular veggies and fruits to make art.
- Model to the children how to hold the different veggies, stamp their flat side into the paint on the plate palette, and then stamp the veggies onto their placemats.
- Invite the children to the stamping table/area. You may need to model the stamping again here.
- Stamp away! Fill the placemats with stamped prints of seasonal fruits and veggies. The children may want to add hand prints (which is super cute), or they may begin to finger paint on their placemats, too.
  - Little hands will get covered in paint, so take the opportunity to add a hand print to the placemat.
  - Hang the placemats to dry. Add the children's names and dates, if you like.
  - Once completely dry, they are washable, and they are a practical item for everyday use at home and school that celebrates a garden harvest and creative connection with nature.

Extensions

- Stamp onto T-shirts, pillowcases, cloth napkins, tea towels, or any other cotton fabric items.
- Stamp onto paper. You can use washable paint for this.
- Make a set of placemats and napkins to be given as gifts.

Rolling Seed Painting

This version of the classic early childhood marble rolling activity rolls it right into the world of nature.

Materials
- A child-size shoebox, brownie pan, loaf pan, or other container with raised sides.
- Round, spherical seeds and bits of nature: walnuts, black walnut pods, acorns without tops, sweet gum balls, sycamore button balls, pecans, oak galls, peach pits, or any other round nut or seed pod collected locally. (There are lots of tropical varieties if you are lucky to live in the tropics.) Store-bought round cracking nuts or round pebbles also work if no round seeds or pods are available locally.
- A bowl for the round nature bits
- Paint - Tempera, washable paints, or even liquid watercolor will work.
- Paper - Card stock is great to use, but construction paper or art paper also works well. The key is that the paper is cut to fit inside the container.
- Optional - Old style ketchup type squirt bottle for thicker paint. Putting the paint into a squirt bottle is an easy way to add paint to the paper once it is in the container, but it isn't necessary.

Preparation
- Go for a nature walk to collect round bits of nature.
- Cut the paper to fit the container.

Procedure

- Gather the children and explore the round bits of nature collected on your walk. Recollect any nature connections made during the collection time. Make sensorial observations on color, texture, and shape of the items. Show pictures of the trees or plants from which these seeds grow to older children.

Demonstrate how to:

- Place a piece of paper into the container.
- Add a couple coordinating colors of paint onto the paper in a squirt or dollop. Depending on the age of the children, this may be a step designated to the adult.
- Add a couple round nature objects to the box.
- Tilt the box back and forth, letting the nature bits roll through the paint and around the box and paper, leaving trails and tracks all around the paper.
- When the child is happy with the look of the paper, or exhausted the rolling process, remove the paper from the box and hang to dry.

Extensions

- Cut pieces of paper to the size of opened cards. Once the children create the rolling seed painting and it is dry, fold the paper into notecards and pair with envelopes. These cards can be collected into stationary sets, and sent as thank you notes, given as gifts, or used any time stationary is needed.
- Scan the paintings and upload to a print-on-demand site to make magnets, calendars, mugs, stamps, totes, or any other items to bring pops of abstract nature creativity to everyday life!

Bird Seed Bagels

I do this activity in winter to attract more wildlife to observe, as well as to explore the ideas of ways humans can help fellow creatures in various seasons. Pairing this project with the extension activity of making "child feeders" makes this both educational and delicious! Use whole-grain bagels to make these hearty snacks more healthy for the creatures, such as raccoons and squirrels, who may eat them after the birds have finished with the seed.

Materials

- Scissors and yarn or twine
- Bagels, halved, I like to use the small size with young children when possible. Many local bagel shops and bakeries are happy to donate day-old bagels; just arrange with them a couple of days ahead of time.
- Large bowl for the bagels
- Vegetable shortening or lard – I call this fat in the lesson.
- Bag of bird seed — if you have nut-allergy children, be sure to check the bag as some have peanuts or peanut oil
- Plastic knives or spoons, or icing spreaders
- Tray/s or pan/s for the bird seed
- A nonfiction children's book about birds.

Allow time for the children to sensorially explore the bird seed. They find great joy in running their hands through the seed, and the children will do this whether you provide them a specific time to do so or not.
I recommend providing time for sensorial birdseed exploration when you first present the bowl of seed, before the seeds and their hands get into the fat, making the seeds stick everywhere.

Preparation

- Arrange the bagels in a bowl, gather spreaders, the fat, and pour the bird seed into the tray/s.
- Cut lengths of yarn approximately 10 inches long.
- Tie the strings around the bagels through the hole so they hang.

Procedure

- Gather the children and engage them in a conversation about any birds noticed lately.
- Have the children close their eyes and listen for birds. Remind them to be silent to carefully hear the birds.
- Read a story to the group and engage students in the lives and needs of birds.
- Explore the role of birds in the garden. How do birds help the garden? Why do we want to attract them? Do you think wildflowers and flowers will attract birds? Why? (Yes, because they provide seeds for the birds to eat.)
- Explain, "Today we are going to make bird feeders to attract birds to our garden."
- Present the bowl or tray of bird seed.
- Pass out the bagels. You may need to remind young children that these are for the birds to eat, not them.

- Demonstrate how to use the spreader to apply fat to the sides of the bagel. If the children are very young, you should do this part for them.
- Model how to dip and press the fat-coated side of the bagel into the bird seed.
- Once the fat is coated in seeds, have the children find places around the garden to hang their feeders.

Extensions

- Bring fresh whole-grain (or gluten-free) bagels, a nut butter or cream cheese spread, and sunflower seeds or trail mix to let the children make "child feeders" for themselves to eat following the same procedure as the bagel "bird feeders".
- Skip bagels all together, and cut heart shapes from up-cycled cardboard. Use the hearts as the base for your bird feeders.
- Make classic pinecone bird feeders.

Cloud Watching

So simple, yet so special, cloud watching is a great way to connect with nature, learn about weather, and spark imagination. When guiding young children to creative nature connections, remember to never underestimate the fundamentals. Cloud watch at different times of day and seasons to observe different types of clouds, as well as different color clouds. Then compare, for example, sunset cloud colors vs. midsummer afternoon cloud colors. Cloud watch on a regular basis. It's as easy as taking a minute to look up at the sky while going from place to place during your regular daily routine.

Materials
- A day with clouds
- An open outdoor space where the sky can be observed
- Blanket/s to lie on
- Nature journals and crayons

Procedure
- Invite the child to lie down with you and look up at the sky. With younger children, you may want to hold them and look up at the sky instead, if lying down isn't practical and they are likely to crawl or run away.
- Provide some quiet observation time, then begin to casually engage the child with observations and questions about the clouds: Look at those big clouds! What color are they? Do you think they will bring rain? Why? Do you see any shapes in the clouds? They sure are moving fast/slow. I see a …. in the clouds. Do you? What do you see?
- Encourage the child's observations and imagination.
- If the child has started nature journaling, present the journal and crayons, and draw pictures of the clouds. If the child is interesting in writing, include names of what she saw in the clouds.

Extension
- Sculpt clouds from white, light blue, and gray play dough
- With ages 4-6, begin to talk about the basic types of clouds, their names, and what type of weather they bring.
- Paint clouds after cloud watching, and tell stories about what you saw in the clouds. Then, read books on weather and clouds once the child's imagination has been sparked.

What nature whisper catches your wonder most easily?

Butterflies, flowers, seeds, waves, clouds, birds...

Share your wonder for that little whisper with a child!

Ladybug Thumbprints

As far as "bugs" go, ladybugs are in the most popular and least scary category. That fact makes them great introductory insects for young children. So what better bug to choose to learn the basic anatomy of an insect than a ladybug? These ladybug thumbprints can be made into bookmarks (my favorite), added into collages, drawings, or paintings of the garden, used to decorate envelopes, or stamped to adorn about any paper surface you can imagine. Young children will need an adult to add the details, but they get the hang of the finger stamping surprisingly quick and enjoy it very much.

Materials

- Red stamp pad
- Black color pencil or thin marker
- Paper

Preparation

- Decide what these thumbprints will adorn, from a nature journal page to a decorative bookmark to card to anything you imagine, and cut the paper accordingly.

Procedure

- Gather the children and read a story, or initiate a conversation using photographs about ladybugs. If you have live ladybugs, show them as well.
- Explore the basic parts of a ladybug and insect: Head, thorax, abdomen, two antennae, six legs, and four wings. Use your own body, and invite the children to touch theirs to learn the parts of the insect as you say them: touch your head (head), touch your ribs (thorax), touch your stomach (abdomen), use two fingers to make antennae on your head, wave your arms and legs for six legs, and bend your arms in to make wings. Repeat the parts and movements. Never fear using the anatomical names. Remember, children ages 3-6 like to use the technical terms and try to say them. This increases nature vocabulary in all children, regardless of whether they remember the names at this stage.

- Present the paper to be stamped and say, "Now we will make pictures of ladybugs and their body parts."
- Show the children how to make a stamp print with their index finger or thumb. Toddlers will likely need you to manipulate their hand at first to teach them how to press their finger into the stamp pad and then press it onto the paper.
- Demonstrate:
  - Draw a line down the center of the thumbprint
  - Add dots to the red abdomen/thorax
  - Add a black semicircle for the head
  - Add two antennae
- Make as many ladybug thumbprints as you like!

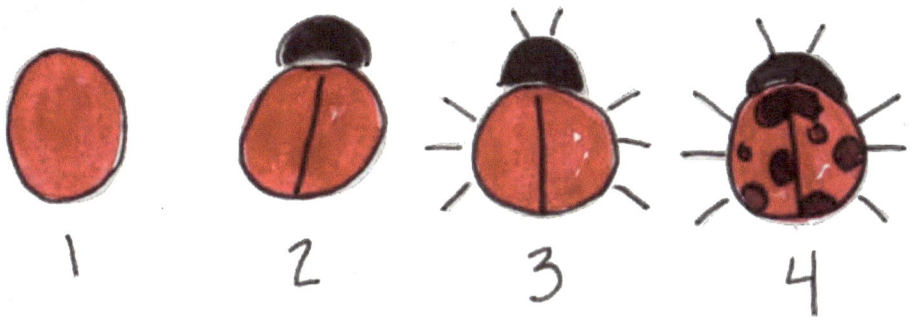

Extensions
- Make ladybug thumbprints on name tags or gift tags.
- In the nature journal, have the child (or the adult, depending on the age of the child) draw a ladybug habitat that has food and shelter for the ladybug based on information learned from a children's ladybug book. Then, invite the child to add thumbprint ladybugs to the habitat.
- Ladybug bookmarks:
  - Cut strips of card stock into 1 x 6-inch strips
  - Punch a small hole about 1/4 inch down from the top of the strips. (I like to use a star shape punch).
  - Give each child a strip on which to make ladybug thumbprints.
  - Once the ladybug thumbprints are complete, tie a thin ribbon to the top to make a bookmark.
  - These are great to use in chapter books being read aloud to the 4-6 age child or to give with book gifts.

Winter Wonder Clay

Play clay has been a childhood favorite for generations. I do this activity with my classes in winter as a way to bring awareness to the wonder-filled bits of nature all around, even when the ground is covered in snow. For everyone who lives in places without snow, this project gives you some "snow day" fun.

Materials
- Winter nature items: seed pods, evergreen sprigs, acorn tops, small twigs, and any other winter nature items local to your area. Fresh store bought herbs, such as rosemary sprigs, can also be used.
- Bright White Play Clay

Bright White Play Clay Recipe
Makes approximately enough for 10 children to have an adult handful-size ball, or fewer children to have bigger portions.

- 4 cups cornstarch
- 2 cups salt
- 4 Tbsp oil (I like to use coconut oil because it smells great.)
- 4 Tbsp cream of tartar
- 4 cups boiling (or nearly boiling) water
- Optional: Three drops of peppermint essential oil. (This is concentrated, so very little is needed. Avoid direct contact with eyes.)
- Mix all of the dry Bright White Play Clay ingredients in a cooking pot.
- Mix in the oil and water and combine. Heat on the stovetop over medium-low heat.
- Stir regularly until the play clay gets thick and comes together in dough consistency.
- Remove from the heat and knead it until smooth and soft, adding in a few drops of peppermint essential oil if desired. If the play clay is too sticky, add a little more cornstarch.

Preparation
- Take a walk in nature to collect small bits of winter nature.
- Make the Bright White Play Clay. This can be done ahead of time, with or without the child involved.

Procedure
- Talk all about snow and the habits of plants and animals in winter. (See Resource section for winter children's stories.)
- Offer the basket or bowl of winter nature items. Sensorially explore each item, naming it and bringing awareness to various aspects of each item.
- Give each child a chunk of Bright White Play Clay. (I like to give each child a tray for their clay play.)
- Let the children sculpt, craft, and create with the "snow" Bright White Play Clay, adding in bits of winter nature.

Extensions
- Make snow humans and snow animals seen on winter walks or read about in winter books, and adorn with bits of nature.
- Use snowflake shape cookie cutters for snow themed play
- Add silver edible glitter to the play clay to make your snow sparkle. (* I recommend the edible glitter because regular plastic glitter is not good for ocean environments, and young children may also try to eat the clay.)

Snow Medallions

Make your nature snow clay creations more permanent with this recipe. It makes about twenty 2-inch diameter medallions.

Materials
4 cups flour
1 cup salt
1 1/2 cups water, add up to 1/2 cup more if the dough is too dry
1 or 2-inch round cookie or biscuit cutter
Optional: ribbon, acrylic paint

Procedure
* Mix the dry ingredients, add the water, and knead vigorously for 10 minutes. This is important to toughen up the dough.
* Roll out the dough, and use cookie or biscuit cutters to make shapes.
* Poke a hole near the top for a hanging string.
* Press bits of nature into the medallions to make patterns and impressions.
* Bake at 325 degrees Fahrenheit until hard, checking at 10 minutes. Let cool and air dry another 24 hours.
* Paint with acrylic paint, if desired. White, silver, glitter and iridescent light blue paints go well with the snow nature theme.
* Add ribbon to hang the medallions in a window, from a tree, or anywhere you like!

Wander

Wander in Both Mind and Body

A huge part of nature connection in early childhood is wandering — without agenda —while letting nature's wonders guide the way. This means lots of walks at the child's pace, going out in all weather and seasons, asking open-ended questions, listening to nature's whispers by noticing the most obvious and often overlooked aspects of common nature, daydreaming, gazing out windows, providing physical and mental freedom for the child to wonder in fascination, and being truly present as the child points out discoveries to you. It means allowing for space and time let the *mind and body* wander in open-ended creative play, exploration, and daydreaming. To wander isn't to be aimless, it's intentionally allowing space in life's busy schedule to let creativity and wonder grow.

When physically wandering, as you walk through nature with the young child (or stroll with the very young child), remember to keep it natural. By natural, I mean don't feel as if you have to point out the name of everything the child picks up or looks at to make the walk meaningful and educational. Just being there walking and expressing interest and wonder is enough for the young child.

If it feels natural to point out something or to offer an object's name, do so. If not, don't, it's okay. Simply enjoy nature's colors, textures, and environment led by the child. (Although, as previously mentioned, do teach the child how to use caution when exploring unfamiliar plants.) If something piques your own interest, remember it and research it when you return home. It's the wonder of discovery that solidifies an interest in nature for the child, not just a name. When names of plants and animals are taught naturally and experientially, it's amazing how many nature names a very young child will remember and pronounce in the most adorable ways.

Stay 2 Steps Ahead

Many of the activities in this section require walks to collect nature items, provide opportunities for hands in the garden soil, and may require a change of clothes, so make sure to prepare accordingly to set the experience up for success. Front end preparation of the adult and the environment (when possible) is huge for a meaningful experience for the child on the back end. Always think two steps ahead, troubleshoot depending on time of day, season, and weather forecast, and be as ready for anything as you can.

Keeping a grab-and-go nature adventure tote stocked and ready is a great way to stay prepared. Keep in it everything you may need to avert disaster, from diapers and wet wipes to band-aids to snacks to umbrellas to even a sling type baby carrier just in case a toddler gets tired of walking. If the season is summer and you are going out in the morning, think water, hats, and sunscreen; at dusk, think bug spray, as the mosquitoes and gnats will likely be out, and maybe a light sweater for when the temperature drops. This type of preparation for nature outings will make them fun and easy for everyone, and help avert meltdowns, which allows everyone to relax and immerse in the wonder-filled process of wandering.

Careful planning and preparation also helps the adults reconnecting with nature be more relaxed, as well. Do remember, even the most tame nature is still wild and can surprise you with an unpredicted rainstorm or unexpected garden creature. Stay safe, keep calm, think practically, go with the flow, try to temper any alarm or fear so as not to spread it to the children, and use your best firm, **and calm,** voice if you need them to act quickly for safety reasons. Keep these tips in mind while wandering, and you'll handle anything nature throws at you with flying colors!

You may want to create a Wander Journal to document your wandering with children adventures. This will help you refine your wandering preparedness and build your confidence and expertise for future adventures. Consider recording the:

- Date and time of day
- Weather
- Location
- Activity (trail walk, canoe ride, beach stroll, park jaunt, etc.)
- What you packed in your tote
- Additional supplies you wish you packed in your tote
- Child behavior (Was the day windy and how did that affect the child's behavior? Were they tired? What engaged them?)
- Ideas for future wandering that came to mind while on the adventure.

Slow Down

Justifying mental wandering, a.k.a. daydreaming or spacing out, can be a challenge in modern life, but with the right planning, it can be one of the best parts of the day. Schedule open time into each day, and week, in varying lengths – and protect it fiercely. Turn off all the electronics, light up toys, media, and social chatter during this allotted time. Invite in the quiet and solitude.

Daydreaming with young children can consist of simply lounging on a blanket staring up into the tree tops for 30 minutes. Let the breathe slow and deepen and the mind wander. Let thoughts drift by like the clouds, not getting involved with the to-dos of the day. A toddler likely won't stay on the blanket, but let the child meander with as little conversation and intervention as is safe. Model peaceful "being" in nature and the child will settle.

Offer older children the freedom to get "bored," and then let them figure their own way out of it.* Reply to a complaint with a simple, "Okay or "Go outside," if you aren't already. Offer nature and art supplies, but not ideas. Model sitting quietly and relaxing. Invite them to sit with you in the shade and unwind. Children quickly become accustomed to mental wandering time and look forward the break from the over stimulation of modern life.

Wandering is one of the most important aspects of building a foundation of nature love in early childhood. The activities in this section offer you many ideas for adding structure, educational assimilation, and creative connection fun to follow up your wandering adventures. These activities often include wandering walks to gather the materials needed for the activity, but they are not meant to replace time scheduled for simple free wandering with the child in natural environments big and small, wild and tame, mind and body. Simply touch, smell, look, pick, jump, splash, climb, hang, swing, and let wandering in the natural world feed the wonder of the human child.

"We are star stuff, keep looking up."

~Neil deGrasse Tyson

---

* Learn more about the benefits of letting kids get "bored": https://www.huffingtonpost.com/dr-vanessa-lapointe/why-you-should-do-nothing_b_9818144.html

Outdoor Color Games

Observing color is a key part of connecting with nature. Even in an area that seems only green, if you really take a few minutes to look, you'll notice how many shades of greens, yellows, and browns are actually present. Color signals safety and danger, seasonal changes, that night or dawn is coming, and that a harvest is ripe to both humans and animals. Color offers uncountable clues that tap us into the cycles of the natural world, so it's never too early to explore color outside! This idea provides a few different activities for connecting with color in creative ways that you can expand upon and adapt to fit the ages of your children, as well as environment and seasons.

Most of these games use color cards. These are simply cards that are flat colors. Color cards can be made from approximately 6 x 6-inch squares cut from construction paper and laminated or swatches of cloth or felt. A drawstring bag (or mystery bag, as I call it) that fits the color cards is a practical way to store them, and allows for mystery drawing of the colors without the children being able to see inside. They love the excitement of drawing from the mystery bag.

"Color is a power which directly influences the soul."

~ Wassily Kandinsky

Color Hunt

This is a great activity for 18 months to 4-year-old children.

Materials
- Color Cards
- Mystery Bag

Preparation
- Choose an appropriate and contained outdoor environment in which the children can safely roam independently and explore color.

Procedure

- Gather outside in a designated spot, on a blanket for example, and engage the children in a conversation about the colors that can be found in the environment.
- Invite a child to pull a color card from the pouch and hand it to you.
- Talk about the color drawn from the bag, and then encourage the children to find that color within the boundaries of the environment. Explain those boundaries, if needed.
- With older children, talk about and observe color subtleties and shades of colors they may find.
- Walk around the area and acknowledge each child's color discovery or help them find an example of the color, if needed. Bring the color card with you, and place it next to the natural item found by the child. Verbalize observations of the child's natural item, the color, and even name the item if possible or appropriate.
- Invite the children to return to the gathering spot. Repeat the game as long as interest is held.

Color Transporting

This is a great activity for 18 month to 3-year-old children. The basic idea is for the child to move the color jug to the matching, or not, colors in the environment, both human and natural. This activity is excellent for balance while walking while holding heavier items, and becoming aware of color in their environment — both human made and natural.

Materials

- Color Cards
- Jugs of colored water coordinating with (some of) your color cards. These can be made using up-cycled gallon jugs or 2-liter plastic bottles or any other jug that can be securely sealed. Fill the jug with water and then add a couple of drops of food coloring. I recommend taping the lids to really secure them because pouring out the water can be very tempting.

Preparation
- Decide how many colors you want to use and make the jugs accordingly. Three different colors often works well. You can use multiple cards and jugs of the same colors if you like.
- Choose an appropriate and contained outdoor environment in which the children can safely roam independently and explore color.
- Place a few color cards around the environment next to natural items of the same color, if possible.

Procedure

There are many different ways that this game can be played and the jugs moved around the environment. Use the ideas here as a jumping off point for your own.
- Gather outside in a designated gathering spot, on a blanket for example, and engage the children in a conversation about the colors that can be found in the environment.
- Place a jug of colored water on top of or next to the corresponding color card. There should be one jug for each child participating in the game, and more color cards than jugs.
- Invite each child to stand next to a color card and jug in the environment.
- Then, invite the children to move their color jug to the color card in the environment. You also can have a child draw a color card from the pouch. For example, say, "Move a green jug to a yellow card," or "Everyone take your color jug to a blue card,"
or "Take a red jug to a red card."

Nature's Spectrum Seek & Find

This is a great activity for 4-to 6-year-old children.

Materials
- A color copy or printout of the Spectrum Seek & Find page for each person playing. Having the page in color is important for children who are not yet reading.
- Double-sided tape
- Nature that can be picked
- **Optional:** harvesting scissors and a small basket

Preparation
- Stick a piece of double-sided tape on each colored line on each page. This may need to be done on site if making pages for more than a couple of children, as once the pages are taped, they can no longer be stacked.

Get a printable pdf of the Wings, Worms, and Wonder "Spectrum Seek and Find" in the "Garden Party" webpage. Find the log-in information on page 4!

Procedure
- Gather outside in the backyard, garden, or other picking permitted nature spot (where there are no known dangers).
- Explain to the children about picking gently in nature and asking before picking unfamiliar things. Offering each child a small basket to carry scissors and to collect harvests is a good way to avoid any walking-with-scissors dangers.
- If you choose to use harvesting scissors for gentle picking, remind them of scissor safety while walking and cutting.
- Engage the children in a conversation about the colors that can be found in the environment.
- Show the children the Spectrum Seek & Find page, and explain that they will each get a page to collect bits of nature that match each color. Show the sticky tape in each section.
- Invite them to explore the environment by collecting pieces of flowers, leaves, feathers, rocks, shells, skins, or whatever other bits of nature found in the colors being sought, and stick them to the spectrum.
- After you are finished collecting, regroup and discuss your color finds.
- Ask: What colors were the easiest to find in nature items? What colors did you find more difficult to discover? Where in nature or in what climate do you think these challenging colors may be easier to find? What tints, shades, and different variations of the colors did you find (ex. pink is a variation of red)? What did you observe and discover while seeking and finding the various colors? What do you observe about the colors and nature items (textures, details, smells, etc.)? Do you know the names of any of the plants or the species of animal? Discuss anything and everything else that comes up.

Seek and Draw Nature Journal Color Study

This activity is version of a drawing scavenger hunt and is best for 4-to-6-year-old children.

Materials

- Nature journal
- Crayons, color pencils, or markers
- Color cards
- A mystery bag
- **Optional:** Clipboards to use as a firm drawing surface

Procedure

- Pull, or have a child pull, a color card from the drawstring pouch.
- Discuss what items of his color can be found in the surrounding natural environment.
- Pass out a crayon (or other drawing material) of the chosen color to each child.
- Encourage the children to go into the environment to discover a natural item of the chosen color and draw it in their journal.
- Return to the meeting area, pull another color card, and draw again.

"Those who contemplate the beauty of the Earth find reserves of strength that endure as long as life lasts.."

~ Rachel Carson

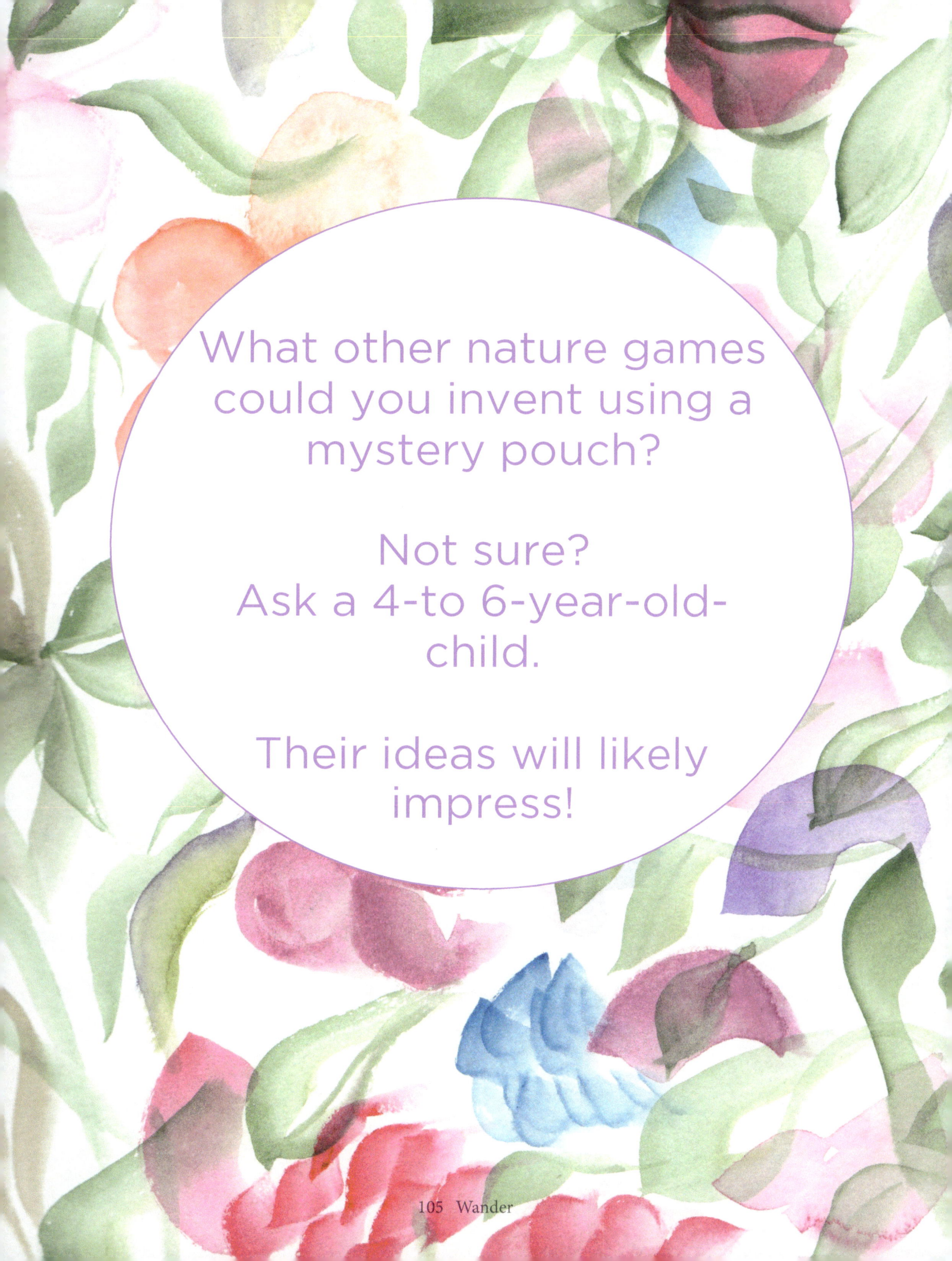

What other nature games could you invent using a mystery pouch?

Not sure?
Ask a 4-to 6-year-old-child.

Their ideas will likely impress!

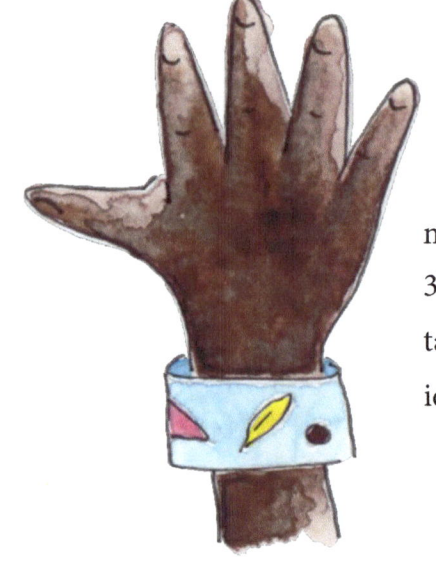

Nature Bracelets

This project idea was adapted from an activity one of my nephews did years ago in his toddler school. Keeping a group of 2- and 3-year-olds together on a nature walk in the city is quite admirable and takes some creativity for sure, so his brilliant teachers came up with the idea of nature bracelets to add focus to their walks.

Collecting items keeps the children engaged with nature while on the walk and also meets the fundamental human need of aestheticism/art/adornment. This activity gets the children observing their natural world by seeking out little whispers and treasures to add to their bracelets. The bracelets also help initiate conversation with the children about the nature they see each day. Make these bracelets while out on a walk, or exploring in the school yard. Alternately, bring a bowl of dried flowers, leaves, herbs, and any other small lightweight nature items indoors, and offer it as an independent nature-inspired art activity.

Materials
- 1.5 to 2-inch wide masking tape, color of your choice.
- For indoor bracelet making – A bowl or sorted bowls of nature items, such as seeds, seed pods, flowers, herbs, leaves, grass, and any other interesting items in your area

Preparation
- If practical, cut the tape ahead of time into approximately 6-inch strips, although this could vary depending on the size of the child. Cut lengths that give ample overlap room so the bracelet stays stuck together on the child's wrist. (Usually, I eyeball the tape for the individual child cutting while outside.)
- Decide on your nature walk route.
- For indoor bracelet making, set up the work at a table, and, if desired, sort the different types of items into separate bowls or baskets from which the children can choose.

Procedure

- Explain to the children that they will each get a sticky bracelet that they can press found nature items onto to make a nature bracelet and piece of art. Explain the parameters of your specific walk, environment, and situation. Also explain what type of items are appropriate to stick, and what are not, if necessary.
- Wrap a length of tape — sticky side out — around each child's wrist.
- Head out on your walk to collect and create beautiful nature bracelets!
- Once you return, the children can continue to wear the bracelets, or cut them off for a little nature art piece.
- Indoor bracelet making: Model making the bracelets by sticking bits of nature to the tape, and offer the lesson at a table independently for children to create.

Extensions

- Older children may be interested in creating a repeat pattern on the bracelet.
- Mount the bracelet onto card stock or glue into the nature journal and add the date and location if you'd like to formalize the work.
- Encase in wide clear packing tape, contact paper, or laminate, and turn into a bookmark.

Ice Catchers

Water play is always a hit with young children, and this activity is no exception because water play in winter adds the process of freezing. Making Ice Catchers allows the child to explore how different items from nature sink or float. They also experiment with the states of matter, learning that liquid water will turn to solid water (ice) when it is cold enough. * If you live where it stays warm all year, use the freezer to do this activity.

Materials
- Natural items, such as leaves, sticks, pebbles, buds, acorn tops, etc., collected on a nature walk
- Ribbon, yarn, or string – 1 piece for each ice catcher, about 8-12 inches long
- Flat bottom shallow containers, such as sandwich-size plastic containers in circle or square shapes – 1 for each child
- Water in a pitcher
- Freezing temperatures or a freezer

Preparation
- Go for a walk with the children and collect various small items from nature.
- Tie the ends of the string together to make a circle. This will be the loop to hang the catcher.
- Talk with the children about what it means to sink or float. Also, you may want to explain what sun catchers are, show a traditional one in a sunny window, and explain that you are going to make one in nature – or even do the Sun Color Catchers activity first.
- If you are doing this with very young children (2 and under), just get outside, no explanation.
- If you are doing this activity with children 4 and older, tie it to a science lesson. Explain how this project illustrates two states of matter (solid and liquid). Provide an opportunity to explore the states. Using very hot water outside on a cold day, demonstrates the third state of matter, gas, with the steam.

Procedure

- Once the children have collected their natural items, offer them the containers in which to arrange the items.
- Before the water is poured, review sinking and floating to the children and explain that the lighter items will move around when the water pours in, but they can rearrange them. Notice how floating items want to group together. (This demonstrates the law of attraction.)
- Pour some water into the container. Depending on the age of the child, they can do this or you can. The container should be about 1/4 to 1/2 full of water.
- Add in the string loop. Make sure a part of the loop is submerged in the water so it will freeze into the catcher. Also, be sure a good part of the loop is not in the water so there will be a loop from which to hang the ice catcher later.

- Place the container outside on a flat surface and let it freeze overnight. If it is really cold where you live, it may not take that long to freeze solid. If you are somewhere warm, put the container into the freezer overnight.
- Once fully frozen, remove the catcher from the container. If needed, run the container under water to loosen the ice from the container, just like you would an ice tray.
- Gently pop the catcher out of the container, and hang it outside to admire from a tree, bush, porch, or on the outside of a window using a suction cup.

Extensions

- Add watercolor paint to swirl color around your ice catcher.
- Icy Bird Feeders. This is great for early spring when temperatures fluctuate between warmer in the day and freezing at night. Create ice catchers using lots of birdseed in water. (Festively shaped silicon molds can be fun for this activity.) Let the icy bird seed shapes freeze outside overnight. The next morning, hang the frozen bird seed feeders in a tree. When they melt the following day, as the sun warms, the seed will drop to the ground and feed the birds!
- With 4-6 year olds, approach these ice catchers as an art project. Use it as an opportunity to talk about basic design elements (symmetry, rule of thirds, central composition, overlapping, and grouping items). Look at picture books with the artwork of Andy Goldsworthy to see how he uses ice and nature to make ephemeral sculptures.

Seed Tapes

Making seed tapes is truly fun for all. I've done this project with children ages 18 months – 12 years, and they all enjoy it equally. Seed tapes are also an interesting way to help people with impaired motor skills plant seeds more easily.

Materials

- Thin cheap construction paper. Newsprint can be used too, just not the glossy pages.
- Scissors
- All-purpose flour
- Water and a bowl
- Cotton Swabs
- Various seed pods and their flowers (if possible)
- **Optional:** Little bowls and trays; paper plates; plastic bags

Preparation

- Cut the construction paper into approximately 1-inch strips
- Make the wheat paste (Papier-mâché paste):
- Mix 1 cup of flour with plain water to make a paste the consistency of a milkshake. Add the water a little at a time, and adjust the flour ratio if it gets too runny. This mix stores well in a sealed container in the fridge for about a week.

THE SCOOP

This wheat paste mix stores well in a sealed container in the fridge for about a week. Simply sir when ready to use.

Procedure

- Go to the garden and collect seeds, or use store-bought seed packets. Small seeds work best, including, but not limited to: radish, basil, lettuce, marigold, and small sunflower (not mammoth). Experiment with various seeds: veggie, flower, and wildflower.

- Show the children how seeds grow from a flower by pulling apart a flower to explore the parts and discover the seeds. (Marigolds are my favorite seed pods for illustrating the seeds within the flower.)
- If using seeds from seed pods harvested from your own garden, show the children how to remove the seeds from the flower head or dried seed pod, and place them in a little bowl.
- (If doing this with children under 3, collecting flowers and removing the seeds may be enough for one day or session, so you could stop here, and continue with making the seed tapes the next day.)

- Place a strip of construction paper on a paper plate.
- Dot the papier-mâché paste onto the strip. Make the dots fairly thick so the seeds will really stick. They don't need to be evenly spaced or even neat, and they won't be when young children make them, but that's okay.
- Add seeds into the paste dots. You could make a pattern or go wild style!
- Set the paper plates aside to let the seed tapes dry completely.
- Then, plant the strips in the garden or in a flower pot.
- If you'd like to save the seed strips for a longer period of time, once they are completely dry, store in sealable plastic bags until ready for planting. The "shelf life" of the seed tapes makes this a good activity to do in winter with seeds harvested the previous fall, and then plant the following spring. As long as the tapes stay absolutely dry, the seeds will be viable for about a year, or as long as the date on their specific purchase package states.

Extensions

- Make seed cards. Cut and fold sheets of construction paper into note-card size and shape. Have the child decorate the card with color pencils or crayons, and then dot the papier-mâché paste and add seeds to the card. Once dry, send to your favorite friend with a little note to plant the card!
- With children 4-6-years-old, before making the seed tapes (possibly on a previous day), study flower heads and seed pods. Remove seeds from the pods, and document findings in the nature journals. Draw and label the entries to create a beautiful page about seeds.

Seed Coats

Did you know seeds wear coats to keep them warm just like us? Exploring the parts of a seed is usually an activity reserved for older children, but when approached on a sensorial level, it is perfect work for early childhood that engages focus and dexterity, while teaching about the powerhouses of nature — seeds! This activity is great fun for children as young as 18 months.

Materials
- Lima bean seeds, dry from a grocery store's dried bean section
- A bowl
- Water
- **Optional:** Parts of a Seed Card Material

Preparation
- Soak about 1/4 cup of dry lima bean seeds overnight. (Depending on the number of children, you may want to soak more. Young children really enjoy peeling lots of seed coats!)
- The soaked seeds can be kept in a sealed container in the fridge for about a week.

Procedure
- Engage the children in a conversation about coats. Ask if they wear coats, why they wear coats (to keep warm and dry). Ask, "Did you know seeds wear coats?" Then explain why a seed would wear a coat for the same reasons a child would wear a coat (to keep safe and warm, to protect its body), and read a book about seeds.
- Present the bowl of soaked lima bean seeds. Explain that all these seeds are wearing coats, and we are going to take off the coat and see what's inside.

- Show the child how to rub the outside of the seed between their fingers to loosen the seed coat, then peel it off completely.
- Explore the thin coat off the seed, notice the texture, thickness, and how the coat wrapped around the seed just the way our coats wrap around us.
- Next, examine the inside of the seed. It has two cotyledon, which is the food for the baby plant growing inside. (These are the two halves of the bean.)
- If they haven't already, split the two cotyledon in half, and discover the tiny leaves and little root growing at one end of the seed. Remove these, and examine the tiny little leaves and root comprising the plant embryo.
- Offer the children the rest of the bowl of soaked beans to peel the coats and remove the baby plants independently, as well as a bowl or tray in which to place the discarded parts of the seed.
- Children may be interested in orally exploring and tasting or eating some or all parts of the soaked bean seeds. This is totally fine and safe — assuming very young children are under the watchful eye of an adult, to avoid any choking risk. They won't taste delicious like when the beans are cooked though.
- **Optional:** Print or copy the Parts of a Seed 3 part cards. Match the parts of the lime bean with the card matching material and record in the nature journal with children ages 4 to 6.

Get a printable pdf of the Wings, Worms, and Wonder "Parts of a Seed" card material from the "Garden Party" webpage.

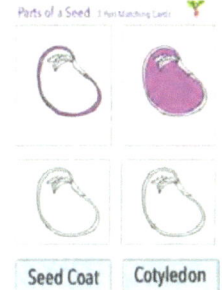

Find the log-in information on page 4!

Extensions

- Save some soaked lima bean seeds and sprout them in the garden or in a clear cup to see the roots grow down, and the shoot grow up. For this, use seeds that have not split once soaked.
- Explore different shapes of various larger seeds, such as: corn, lima bean, pea, pumpkin, and avocado. Then, plant them in a garden or in flower pots.

Nut Cracking Work

This was a favorite activity of the children in my very first toddler class. Even the ones who wouldn't eat the nuts loved to crack them and feed them to the other children. This work is excellent for fine motor development.

Materials
Nuts to crack:
Almonds, Paper Shell Pecans,
Peanuts in the shell
(dry roasted or boiled)
A child friendly twist style nutcracker
(See Resources)

Procedure
Explain how the nuts we eat are also seeds. Show the children how to open or crack nuts and eat the seeds.

Organic Peanuts in the shell (dry roasted or boiled) are excellent to introduce young children (18 months and up) to nut cracking work, if it is confirmed the children are not allergic. The shells of peanuts are easily opened with just the fingers. Then, progress to using a twist style nut cracker for cracking paper shell pecans, almonds, and even walnuts, as the children master various shells.

Re-Grow Gardening

This is perhaps the easiest gardening around — re-growing your veggies! This super-simple gardening project is great because it doesn't have the wait time that regular gardening does, which is tough for younger children, it is perfect for small spaces, and it doesn't require much beyond the leftovers from lunch or dinner. It's also perfect indoor winter gardening.

Materials
- Easy regrow veggies such as: celery, romaine lettuce, basil sprig, cilantro sprig, potatoes, sweet potatoes, garlic bulb, onion bulb, scallion/green onion, beetroot top, carrot top.
- Flat-bottom bowls or ramekins of various sizes to place your re-grow veggies
- Warm water
- Small knife and cutting board
- Sunny window with space for the bowls on the sill or on an adjacent table

Preparation
- Choose your veggies or fruits to re-grow.
- Explore the regrowing chart on the following page to see how and where to regrow and replant your produce.
- Make sure you have a container that is slightly larger in circumference of the produce to regrow.

Procedure

- Introduce the various produce you will re-grow. Observe the different aspects of the particular produce, any leaf shapes, colors, textures, and what part we eat.
- Show the full vegetable or produce, and then cut off the part you will eat (now or later) and set aside. (Depending on the particular piece of produce, like with carrots for example, you may snack on the edible part of the produce as part of the lesson.)

- Explain how we can grow more of the produce with the leftover parts. We don't always re-grow the same part we eat, but we can regrow the plant.
- Based on the information provided in the chart, show the children how to "plant" the portion of the veggie to re-grow into the warm water, or, in some cases, a flower pot with soil. Planting is simply setting the portion of the produce into the container with about 1/2 inch of water, cut side facing down into the water. (See chart and illustration.)
- Set in a sunny window, keep watered, and watch them re-grow! Once root and/or leaf growth is apparent, replant into a pot or the garden, if you like.

Extensions

- Sprout an avocado seed on toothpicks in the kitchen or classroom. Insert 3-4 toothpicks into the sides of the bottom third of the seed with portion below the toothpicks submerged in the cup of water.
- Make sure the water stays touching the seed bottom.
- Once it sprouts, and you see the first leaves, move it to a sunny window.
- Plant it in a pot once it has roots and a set of true leaves. (The second set of leaves.)

Produce	How to Re-Grow It
Celery, Romaine, Green Onion	- Cut the bunch about 3-inch up from the base. - Set the base of the plant down into 1/2-inch of water. - Set in a sunny window and wait for new leaves and roots to grow, making sure that there is always water in the container. - Plant into the garden or a pot, burying all but the new leaves and shoots. - Let the plant greens fully grow before re-harvesting.
Basil sprig, Cilantro sprig	- Pick off the bottom most leaves, leaving the very top bunch of leaves intact on the stem. - Cut the bottom of the stem to open up the plant's ability to uptake water — about 1-inch. - You should have around 3-4 inches of stem with small leaves at the top. - Place into a glass of water in a sunny window. - When you see roots grow to about an inch long, plant in a pot. - You can harvest more leaves in about two weeks.
Potato	- Get a potato with "eyes" starting to sprout from the grocery or market. If the potato is large and has lots of "eyes," cut it in half and plant halves separately. - Plant the potato in a flower pot or in the garden with the eyes facing up in about 4-inches deep in the soil. You can stop here and just grow a potato plant, or… - Bury the potato at *the bottom* of a large empty flower pot (or in the garden) with the eyes facing up. Cover with about 4-inches of soil, not filling the pot. - As the potato plant grows a stalk and leaves out of the soil, add more soil, burying the plant deeper and filling the pot or creating a mound of soil over the plant. As the plant grows and is buried, potatoes will grow from the stalk. Keep covering the plant with soil, leaving only the top bunch of leaves exposed above the soil. - When the pot is full of soil, and leaves start to die back on the plant, it's time to dump the pot or dig the mound and harvest potatoes!
Sweet Potato	- Place a sweet potato vertically into a glass, or vase, of water. You can use three toothpicks inserted into the sides of the sweet potato to suspend half of it above the water line if needed. - Watch for roots to appear growing down and shoots and leaves to grow up. - Let the sweet potato grow as a beautiful vining ornamental indoor plant, or… - Plant it in your garden in early summer with the leaves and shoots above the soil, let them run across the surface of the soil, and in the fall when the leaves die back, dig up more sweet potatoes!
Carrot, Beet	- Cut the bottom main portion off to eat, leaving about an inch of root, plus stalks. If the greens are still attached to the beetroot or carrot, cut them off too, leaving about 1-inch of the stalks. - Place the base in a container of water and set in a sunny window. - Make sure about 1/2-inch of water stays in the container. - Watch for new leaves and roots to grow. - These won't grow new carrots or beets, but they will grow lovely ornamental green tops, and beet greens taste great and are very healthy.
Garlic	- Place a single clove, with skin on, into a container of soil, or directly into the garden, with the point side up. It's really great when you find one already sprouting and can regrow that one. - Keep the soil moist, and let it grow - Harvest the new garlic bulb when the green stalks die back.

Sun Color Catchers

Suncatchers are a beautiful way to invite the color spectrum indoors, but what if the colors come from Mother Nature herself? In this project, collect color from the natural world to incorporate into suncatchers to hang in a window. This activity is best done with children 18 months and older who are walking independently. Children 18 months through 2 years will enjoy doing this activity with an adult.

Materials
- Clear shelf liner paper
- Dessert-size paper plates (approximately 6.5 x 6.5 inches) (I like to use solid-color plates.)
- Access to bits of beautiful nature, such as flower petals; seed pods; leaves; stalks; tiny shells; etc.
- Scissors and/or a circle compass cutter
- Hole punch
- Yarn or ribbon

Preparation
- Cut out the circular centers of the plate, this will be the flat bottom part of the plate.
- Cut the liner paper into squares (or circles) that are larger than the hole in the plate, but smaller than the plate itself. You will need 2 of these for each plate to cover the front and back of the hole like a window.
- Punch a hole at the top of the plate.
- Cut approximately 10-inch lengths of yarn or ribbon.
- Tie the yarn through the punched hole to hang the sun color catcher.
- Stick the clear liner paper to the BACK SIDE of the plate. This means that the sticky side will be showing through the circular window on the front side of the plate.
- Decide on a safe outdoor space, where the child can pick and wander independently, in which to conduct this activity.

Procedure

- Invite the children to gather in the contained and safe nature environment.
- Talk about the sun, feel it shine on your face, hold up a leaf and flower, and observe how the sun shines through it, glowing with color.
- Look around the garden, and notice all of the colors, and point out different leaves and flowers.
- Explain to the children that they are going to make a sun color catcher by picking and sticking different color leaves, flowers, and bits of nature to the clear liner paper.
- Demonstrate how to pick and stick onto a sample sun color catcher. Then, give each child a sun color catcher of her own.
- Encourage the children to explore, picking and sticking to their own sun catchers. Do this with them on your own sun catcher to model the process of exploring around the garden, and how to gently pick from plants.
- Once they have filled the clear window of their sun catchers with nature stuck to the shelf paper, invite them back together to make observations about the items chosen.
- Place the 2nd piece of clear shelf paper over the nature items sticking it to the front side of the plate, securing the nature items within the window.
- Hold the sun color catchers up to the sun and observe how interesting the items now look with the sun shining through. Notice the colors, shadows, veins, and the way some bits of nature let light shine through and others create a silhouette.
- Later, the sun color catchers can be hung in a window to enjoy the beauty of the sun glowing through nature's colors!

Extensions

- Make the picking and sticking a game by calling out various colors and/or items (pick a red leaf, a yellow flower) for the children to find and stick to their sun color catchers.
- Older children can draw a nature pattern around the outer edge of the plate before sticking the shelf paper on, and then also create a pattern within their window using nature.

Leaf Splatter Painting

This is a great activity to introduce children of all ages to abstract expressionism, using nature as the inspiration. This activity, and abstract expressionism in general, reminds us of the a balance between order and chaos that exists across all aspects of life. Young children are in the sensitive period for order, yet life with them as an adult sometimes seem chaotic. When we provide the external order in the environment, it balances the child and nurtures the desire of order she craves in a world so new and big. In this activity, the nature provides the order, the paint provides the chaos, and the sweet spot of balance comes when we remove the nature once the paint is dry to reveal the clear shapes left.

Materials
- Tempera, acrylic, or liquid watercolor paint, two to three coordinating colors.
- Cups or bowls for the paint
- Brushes. Toothbrushes and paintbrushes for creating different effects. (If you really want to get technical, harder grade toothbrushes create a better spray than soft, but whatever you have on hand will work fine.)
- Drawing or painting paper, or any thicker paper that can hold paint — like art, construction, or card stock
- Leaves of various shapes and sizes
- Sticky mounting putty or tape (anything to hold the leaves in place while painting)
- Pieces of cardboard slightly larger than your paper
- **Optional:** Smocks, Protection for a surface you don't want covered in paint

Preparation
- Before painting, take a nature walk and collect a variety of leaves.
- With children 3-6, explore the types of leaves collected, including the shapes and margins of each leaf. (See Resources). These can then be drawn in their nature journals, and become the beginning of an exploration project on a specific type of tree or leaf style. With 2-to 3-year-old children, simply explore the leaves' colors, textures, and shapes.

- Prepare and organize the paint and brushes. Paint should be runny. The thinner the paint, the easier it will spray and flick off the toothbrush, creating more defined edges around the leaves, almost like an airbrush. Toothbrush paint flicking is more for children 5 and up, as it requires a higher level of dexterity. Children ages 2-4 use the brushes in a more traditional manner. Regular paintbrushes can be used to "throw" off paint in a Jackson Pollock style.

Procedure
- Attach the piece of drawing or painting paper to the cardboard. You can use the sticky tack or tape.
- Arrange the leaves and tack them down to the paper so they won't move. Focus on making sure the edges of the leaves are as flat against the paper as possible, so use tiny flattened pieces of sticky tack putty.
- Dip the brush into the paint, and flick paint off the brush onto the paper. (Hint: If using a toothbrush, scrape your thumb over the bristles TOWARD your body, flicking paint onto the paper in a spray. Scraping the bristles away from your body will flick the paint onto you, but that can be fun sometimes too!)
- Encourage a lot of paint to be flicked around the outer edges of the leaves, so the margins come out clearly.
- Once the child is pleased with how the paper is covered in paint, set the art paper aside to dry.

Once dry, remove the leaves and the paper from the cardboard. Enjoy the shapes of the leaves left in the negative space.

Extensions

- Mount the print onto a larger piece of construction paper in a coordinating color as a frame to create a defined border around the print. This juxtaposes a wild style of painting with an orderly and grounded border, thereby creating balance.

- Explore pictures of abstract expressionist painting by artists such as Khalid Thompson, Helen Frankenthaler, Willem deKooning, Joan Mitchell, and Jackson Pollock. Open conversations about what the children see in the paintings, about the colors, and about the movement in the mark making.

- Go big! Tape a large piece of paper to a wall or fence (over a drop cloth, or other protection if you do not want the surrounding area to be covered in paint, too). Tape large leaves to the paper, and fling paint large scale!

THE SCOOP

The process of abstract expressionist painting is great fun, but it can get a bit expressive, a.k.a. very wild and messy, so this is a good activity to do outside.

If at home and the weather is warm, you may even consider allowing the child to paint in the buff, like Jackson Pollack did in his piece "PaintRollerSidewalk!"

At the very least have the child wear a smock or old clothes that can get paint covered to prevent any hinderance on the creative expression.

"A rainy day is the perfect time for a walk in the woods."

~Rachel Carson

Rainy Day Water Play

Is there a child who doesn't like to splash in a puddle? And really, don't we adults want to splash, too, but the day's rush keeps us from such inefficient enjoyment. For true rainy-day and all-season water play, adults have to let go of the ideas of mess vs. clean up, make a good plan, and immerse in the present moment, as hard as this may be to our product-oriented minds. Preparation is key for water play to go smoothly.

Children should have seasonally appropriate clothing for water play: raincoats, rain boots, snow clothes, snow boots, snow gloves, bathing suits, and water shoes. The adults should have a system prepared for cleaning and warming up the child post play. In this activity, explore ideas for water play — whether liquid, frozen, or mixed with soil into mud!

While splashing in puddles, rain and mud, is great for many reasons, it also provides an opportunity to teach the important lesson of "Time and Place" appropriateness. When presenting splashing opportunities, explain to the child why the occasion is appropriate. Then use rainy days out on the town to explain why that time and place is not appropriate for splashing — *before* you encounter the puddles to prevent any issues while out. Stay a splash ahead and puddles are a joy!

All logistics aside, remember the simple joy of a rainy-day walk in nature as Rachel Carson recommends. Get out there! The fun you have will be worth the prep and clean up.

Developmentally, puddle splashing allows children:
- To experiment with the actions and outcomes of jumping and exploring the force of their jump vs. the rise of the splash.
- The opportunity to use their sensorimotor skills (sensory and motor skills) to gain knowledge about their physical environment.
- A beginning understanding of cause and effect.
- Creative problem-solving opportunities and the confidence to independently overcome problems with creative solutions.

Rain Puddle Splashing

So simple, but so often not allowed. Put on the boots, get out there, and splash! Sing splashy rainy-day songs, and enjoy the pure sensorial wonder of a puddle. Puddles show a reflection of the sky, while housing a mystery beneath the surface, and that sky mirror can be shattered with a simple splash. Very young children are amazed at the appearance of the basic puddle itself, and will test it cautiously, and repeatedly, in many ways from tapping a toe to dipping a finger, to wading and making ripples before intuitively going for the big splash (and inevitably tumbling into the water, which is also okay and great fun, too).

Snow Splashing

Snow is a wonder-filled world like no other. A frozen puddle offers great opportunities for exploration: stomp and watch it crack; listen to it crackle when walked upon; pick up pieces and see what happens when they are thrown; see if there is water underneath; is there snow on top; is it slippery or rough to walk on; how much caution is needed to not fall when walking on the ice puddle and how can balance be regained if the child does slip? A slush puddle is equally as fascinating, as it is part liquid, part solid. Bundle up and let frozen puddles guide winter splash play. "There's no such thing as bad weather, only bad clothes," as the Norwegians say!

Mud Splashing

This adult laundry nightmare is a child's pure joy. Letting children splash in mud puddles is a gift to them. Sure, it requires planning and a lot of clean up, but the joy the child gets from exploring the sloppy, sticky, splashy texture of a mud puddle is sensory play at its finest. Offer the child cups, bowls, spoons, funnels, scoops, basting brushes, and pie pans, and let them have a mud kitchen to bake you muddy pies and soups galore. In school environments, it's more practical to schedule mud play days so the children can bring in extra changes of clothes. Each year at the end of June is International Mud Day, where schools and children's centers around the globe celebrate the fun of mud play. (See the Resources section for Mud Day tips.)

Extensions

- **Puddle Painting.** Using a clean puddle, or a small bucket of water, and a house painting size paint brush. Show the child how to use water to "paint" rocks, fences, sticks, trees, and any other object that attracts their attention. They will discover that the water changes the color of the objects, and the sun changes the object back to the original color as the "paint" dries. This activity is especially mesmerizing to children ages 18 months to 3 years. (In some locations and situations water painting can turn into mud painting. It is okay, simply set parameters as to where is appropriate for the child to "paint" with the mud.)

- **Chalk Puddle Painting.** Use sidewalk chalk to draw on a wet sidewalk. The colors will be smooth and vibrant. Scribble vigorously in a shallow puddle to make "paint," then use a paint brush to paint chalk puddle pictures.

- **Mud Pies.** This classic childhood endeavor provides children with the opportunity for imaginative play a la mud. You could even create an entire mud play outdoor kitchen!

- **Snow Painting.** This is a lateral as it sounds. On a snowy day, take watercolor paints outside and paint pictures directly on the snow!

- **Plant Polishing.** After a rain shower take a small cloth and show the child how gently rub, or "polish," a leaf to remove any dust or dirt. This can be done to indoor houseplants or garden plants using a spray bottle. It gives the 3-to 6-year-old child the opportunity to care for her environment, as well as explore up close the textures of leaves and parts of plants.

- **Flower Soup.** Offer the child a bowl or tub of water with flower petals floating in it. (You could leave a bowl out and collect rain water in preparation.) Use fresh petals, dried all natural potpourri, or a mix of both for various textures. Offer a sifter, spoons, and cups. Add natural edible scented waters to increase the sensory exploration. Try rosewater with organic rose petals (fresh or dried), lavender water with lavender sprigs, and orange blossom water with just about everything! Edible scented waters can be found in natural food stores and international food markets and are surprisingly inexpensive. If the child is under 3 or still regularly engaged in oral exploration, make sure your flowers are edible. Flower "soup" can be converted to a snow play activity by using store bought flowers and making flower "cakes" with snow.

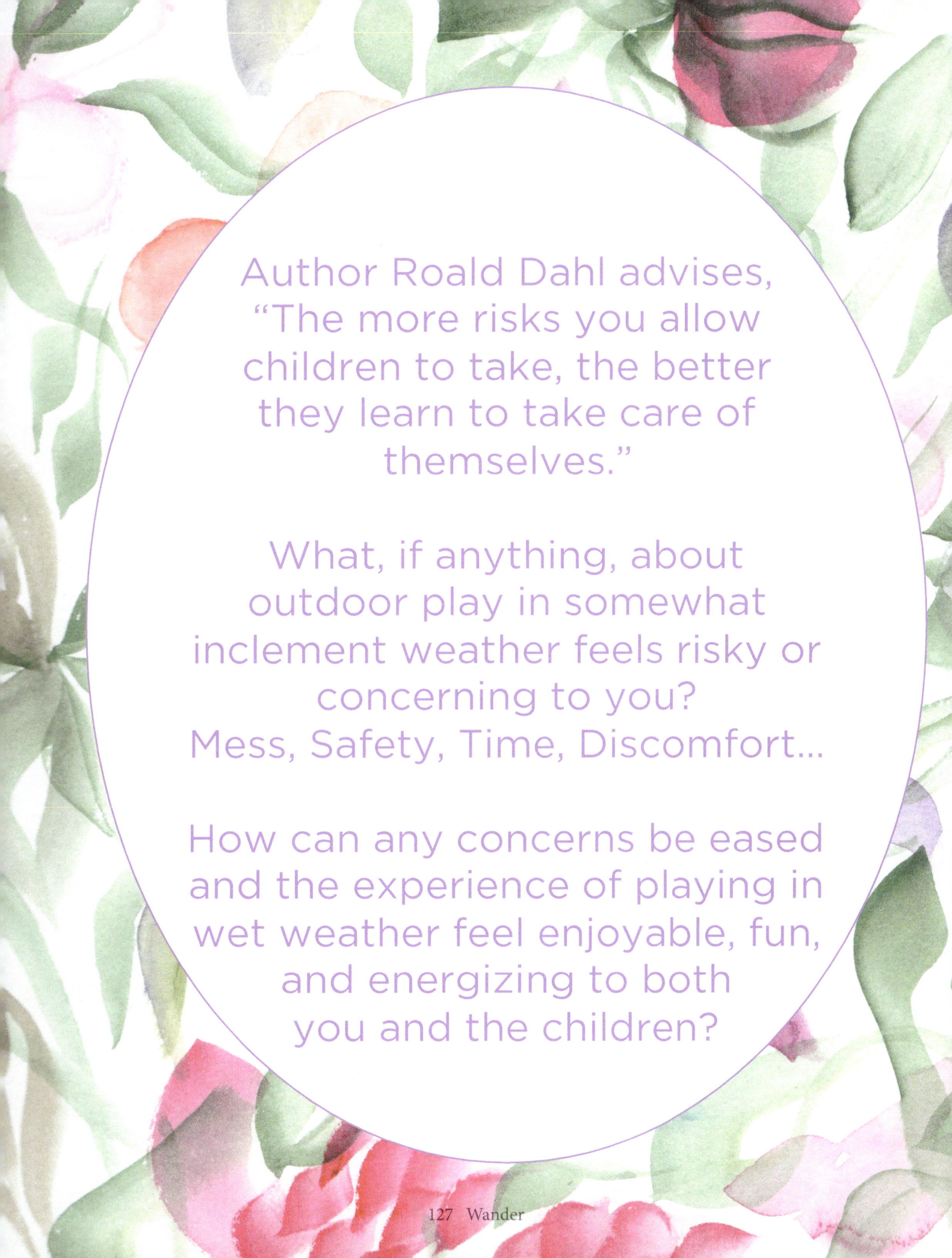

Author Roald Dahl advises, "The more risks you allow children to take, the better they learn to take care of themselves."

What, if anything, about outdoor play in somewhat inclement weather feels risky or concerning to you?
Mess, Safety, Time, Discomfort...

How can any concerns be eased and the experience of playing in wet weather feel enjoyable, fun, and energizing to both you and the children?

Garlands

Garlands are a special way to welcome nature into daily life. Make seasonal nature garlands to celebrate birthdays, solstices, equinoxes, and just about any day you imagine! Pair your garlands with ribbons or colored raffia to add an extra bit of festive flair. Children as young as 18 months enjoy collecting and "sewing" objects onto pieces of yarn, so why stick just to the toy sets of wooden beads? Let children and nature's creative connections supply the decorative backdrops to life events.

The basic materials and process of garland making are the same, regardless of what you string up, so take the ideas below and run with them as suits your environment. The garlands also can be hung indoors or out, depending on what you want to adorn! This activity is best divided into multiple sessions, spread over a couple days, or appropriate to leave out and available for independent work.

General Instructions for Garland Making - Using Leaves

Materials

- Items to string up (leaves)
- Large plastic children's safety needle, or tape or glue put on the end of a piece of yarn in lieu of the needle
- Knife
- Scissors
- String or yarn
- Hole punch, or other hole poking tool
- **Optional:** Ribbons or raffia to tie in between the nature bits, or large beads to string along with the nature

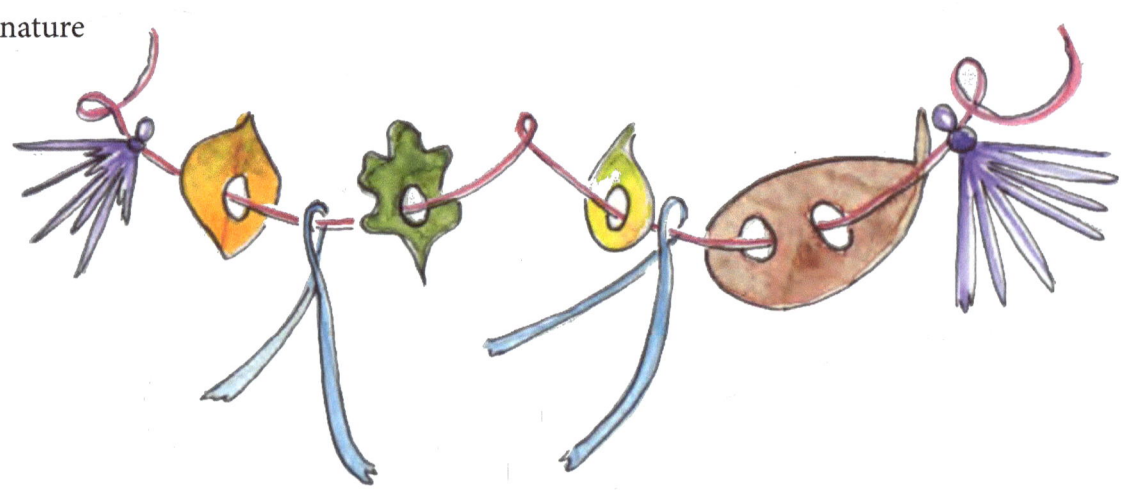

Preparation

- Cut the yarn into lengths. The age of the children will determine the length of the yarn pieces. For children under 3 years, cut the yarn about an adult arm's length. Children older than 3 can handle about two adult arm's lengths once they get the hang of the process. These shorter lengths can later be tied together to form a longer full garland.
- Go on a nature walk to collect the leaves to string.
- Collect leaves of any color. Brown leaves are best strung as full leaves as they are more brittle. Fresh green or fall color leaves can be used full or torn, but are best used within a day or two of collection, as they will become more brittle and wilted.
- Tear the leaves into pieces or use them whole. The tearing of leaves is a very fun activity in and of itself for young children. Most deciduous tree leaves tear into unique shapes along their veins. If tearing leaves, collecting will be one day or session, tearing the next, and garland making follows last.
- Punch or poke holes in the center of the leaves to make them thread-able. You may discover you need more pieces once the threading process begins. I recommend always making more pieces than you think you will need.
- Tie a knot and loop in one end of the string so the pieces don't slide off the end while the child is threading the garland.
- Once the desired number of threading pieces have been collected and holes punched for threading, place the objects to be threaded in a bowl.
- Tie the safety needle onto the yarn with a basic knot to prevent it from falling off and frustrating the child. If using the glue on yarn method, simply dip the end of the yarn into liquid glue and let dry to stiffen.

To make the leaves lie flat along the string, poke two holes into the leaf and thread through both holes. Alternate leaves and beads (or other nature items such as shells, etc., if you want to make a pattern).

Threading Procedure and Finishing

- Demonstrate how to thread the string through the garland pieces, basically sewing them onto the string. Enjoy the process, and make patterns if desired.
  - Once the child has completed her garland threading, remove the safety needle (if using one), and tie a matching knot and loop at the top end.
- If you like, once the garland pieces are secure, tie ribbons and raffia onto the garland to add breezy flair and/or add to more strands to make a longer garland.
- If a child under age 3 does not show interest in the stringing activity, let them do the tearing, and the adult or older children take the lead on the actual garland threading.

Extensions

- **Bird Feeder Garlands.** This is a classic wintertime activity. Make garlands from popcorn and dried fruits to feed the birds in winter. These threading items are tougher and require a sharper metal needle. This is a great next stage for children around age 5 who are skilled enough to safely use a sharper metal needle and thread rather than yarn. I like quilting needles for making these garlands, as they are larger and thicker than regular sewing needles. Cut a length of thread, and string popcorn, raisins, and fresh or dried cranberries into a garland. Older children may like to incorporate a pattern into this style of garland. Hang the garland in a tree or shrub and watch the birds enjoy your edible art!

- **Citrus Garlands.** Collect citrus peels. Use just one variety, or use a combo of peels. Each large navel orange rind has the potential to make approximately three or four two-inch garland pieces. Let the peels sit out on the counter overnight to dehydrate a little bit. This makes the peels a little more leathery, pliable, and less easy to break, but freshly peeled rinds also can be used. Flatten out the peel pieces, and either tear or cut pieces from the peels. Use a cookie cutter at this step if you want to make specific shapes. Thread and finish as instructed above.

Sun Prints

Try this if you have extra leaves left over from your garland making, or from your sun or ice catchers.

Materials
Nature items
Brightly colored construction paper

Procedure
* Place the nature items in a design on top of the paper.
* Leave the paper with the nature on top out in direct sun for two hours during the sun's peak of the day.
* Return to the paper (after lunch and a nap(for example).
* Remove the items
* See how the sun has bleached the paper around the items, leaving an impression of a darker shape where the nature once was.

This also can be done in a very sunny southern-exposure window in winter. Just leave the paper to bleach for a day or so.

Night Nature

Night brings out so many interesting creatures we can't find during the day. From night pollinating moths, to lightning bugs, and even crabs, bats, lizards, and other creatures who eat the night bugs. Nature continues to work her wonder in the shadows of nightfall. In *The Sense of Wonder*, Rachel Carson wrote about sharing "inconvenient" nature with her young nephew Roger:

> "We have let Roger share our enjoyment of things people ordinarily deny children because they are inconvenient, interfering with bedtime, or involving clothing that has to be changed….I think we have felt that the memory…would mean more to him in manhood than the sleep he was losing" (Carson 22).

Forgo bedtime worries now and again to enjoy the wonder that night nature bestows!

Tips for Night Nature Success

Prepare the child for staying up past bedtime. Take a rest (or extra rest) the day of, and tell her she also will rest or go to bed earlier the next day. Explain that she will stay up (or be woken up) at night to observe nature, and that it's not regular play time; it's a special night nature time. If the weather is cold, bundle up in blankets and snuggle outside in the dark while watching the moon and listening to night sounds. (Winter night nature adventures are less bedtime schedule intrusive since it gets dark early.)

Some children may be afraid of the dark, so talk with them about why the dark is scary to them, how if we learn about the night that it makes it less scary, and how you are there to keep them safe. Don't put the idea of night or dark being scary into their heads if it isn't there already. Read books on the creatures you may discover, and talk about the night: Why does it get dark; why do some creatures come out at night; why do the moon and stars shine brightest at night? Once this night nature groundwork is laid, when something amazing happens outdoors at night, like a meteor shower or beautiful lightning, the child can be spontaneously awoken to enjoy it.

Night Nature Activities

Moon Circles and Star Gazing

Moon circles are a clear way to connect children to the phases of nature. The child can easily see how a full moon lights up the sky, and how the sky is dark and great for star gazing during the new moon. Explore the moon shadows that a full moon casts. Notice how our eyes adjust to the dark of a new moon, and how much we can actually see in the dark when we allow our eyes time to adapt. Create a ritual around your moon circles: Make offerings to the moon and stars crafted earlier in the day; sing songs; listen to the night animals; and enjoy a special tea and snack. With children ages 5 and older, begin to include observations of the waxing and waning moon phases in the cycle as well. If you live near an ocean, observe the differences in the tides, and talk about how the moon and ocean are connected through the tides. Bring a blanket or lounge chair, and gaze up at the stars and ponder the cosmos with the children. As Carl Sagan reminded us in his 1973 book *The Cosmic Connection*, "We are made of starstuff."

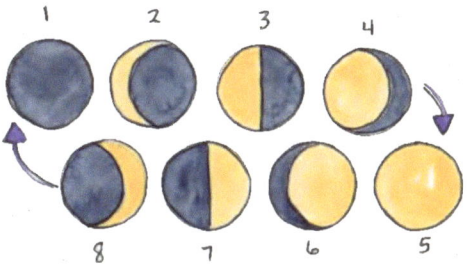

Night Bloom Gardening

Night gardens are not only visually gorgeous as they glow in pale whites, pinks, and blues in the light of the full moon, many night-blooming plants smell wonderful, too, as they attract their pollinators with smell rather than sight.

While some gorgeous night bloomers are toxic, such as plants in the Datura and Nicotiana family, and should be avoided in the gardens for young children, plenty of others are safe. Always check with an expert if you are unsure about a plant's toxicity and appropriateness for growing near young children. Try planting some child friendly night-blooming flowers and see who turns up to pollinate while you swoon over their sweet scents.

Flower	Varieties and Suggestions
Lily	There are a few types of lilies that are scented night bloomers. Plant a few bulbs of the bright white Casablanca lily in the fall to bloom late summer. It does very well in a container, making this flower great for patio or porch gardens. Spider lily makes a sweet-smelling big white flower that has skinny petals that look like spider legs hanging from the center.
Evening Primrose	This does well in poor soils, and blooms from spring through fall, attracting pollinators galore. The yellow flowers open around dusk, and are very drought-tolerant.
Night Jasmine	Is it possible to top the scent of jasmine? Not all varieties are night blooming, but most will smell really great starting in the afternoon. There are many varieties that grow in tropical to temperate zones, so ask a local expert to find the one that grows best in your area.
Four O'Clock	This is one of my personal favorites to grow because they serve double early childhood duty in the garden. The glowing flowers actually do open at about four o'clock in the afternoon. By nightfall, their sweet, dreamy scent fills the air. By day, these prolific self-seeders offer small fingers excellent seed collecting work. Four O'Clock plants are child height and the seeds are a deep black, easy to spot on the plant. They are about the size of a dried pea, and are simply perfect for a child to pick with one hand and place in a small container held by the other. The children in my life regularly ask to come pick seeds in my yard, and I keep little collection jars with their names on them in my garden shed. The seeds can then be shared or spread around the yard, and in any other places you'd like to grow them. You'll only need to buy a pack of seeds once!
Ginger	If you live in a tropical or subtropical zone, there are many night-scented gingers to grow. To start, definitely grow the night-scented butterfly ginger (in my top five favorite garden flowers). The scent is euphoric! The ephemeral white flowers bloom only about 24 hours, but smell for days when picked, and they spread through tubers so you get more each year!

THE SCOOP

More night-blooming flowers to try:
Night-blooming water lilies, Chocolate flower, Night blooming cacti, Hellebore, Heliotrope, Gardenia, Crinum Lily, and Night Scented Orchid.

Extensions

These activities are favorites of some good friends. They can be done in the backyard, schoolyard, campsite, or any other enclosed or semi-enclosed space you deem safe and appropriate for a little independent child to night wander.

- **Bug Buddy Lantern Circles.** Head outside in a safe dark area as a group. Sit together in a circle and shine a lantern or flashlight to see "who" comes to investigate the light. Then, walk around with the light looking for insects. When you find some, observe them in the light, and even follow them if they try to run away to see where they go. Do these night creatures try to hide from the light, or are they attracted to it? Why? What kind of "bugs" are they: beetles, moths, crickets? Are they even insects at all: slugs, lizards, bats? Once this activity is familiar, brave older children may want to venture solo with their own personal lantern or light in an enclosed backyard. Always be sure to join together as a group in a circle before closing the activity to share what types of night creatures were attracted to the light to assimilate the experience.

- **Night Nature Shadow Puppets.** Help each person find a few interesting and beautiful bits of nature. Then, gather at a spot that has a vertical flat surface, such as a wall, fence, or tent side. One person shines the flashlight on the flat surface, while the other/s place their nature objects into the beam. What kind of shadow does the bit of nature throw onto the surface? How does that shadow change as the object is moved closer or farther from the light source? Encourage the child to tell a story, sing a song, or make observations about the shadows made from their objects. This is a great activity to do as a nature-based extension for learning about the traditional art of Indonesian shadow puppetry and oral story telling.

Closing

You are Ready

You have plenty tools, tips, and tricks to set your wondering and wandering up for success. Now, all you need to do is head outside and get started. I've said it many times in the pervious pages, but only because it is so important to remember:

> **Keep it slow,**
> **Keep it small,**
> **Keep it simple.**

With a wonder–filled child, observe industrious ants crawl on the sidewalk, listen to small birds sing from a telephone wire, stop to smell a sweet flower, notice the ephemeral play of light and shadow on the grass, and watch cool raindrops roll down a window. Connect together, letting the day's cares and obligations fade, if only for ten minutes. It's these little experiences that add up to a creatively nature connected life.

As you follow the child, on every walk you take, flower you smell, and nature inspired art you make, nurture the re-blooming of your own sense of wonder. Know you are part of an important movement to build naturalist intelligence, to sprout green thumbs, and to keep humans and nature connected. Each time you create a nature experience for a child, you are making the world a "greener" place for all children's futures.

Rachel Carson said, "Exploring nature with your child is largely a matter of becoming receptive to what lies all around you" (52). Stay open to the joys of wondering and wandering. You will be challenged, but nature will always reward you for the effort. Each activity here is complete, yet also a spring board for your own imagination. Grow them in your own way.

And for those times when you need an extra boost beyond what you found in this guide, I am here to help. Visit Wings, Worms, and Wonder online to contact me and find even more resources, activities, and practical tips to keep your life filled with wonder as you wander.

You are ready to fly from the nest, so gather the children and head outside!

Sincerely,
Kelly

Resources

Wings, Worms, and Wonder

Books

- *Wings, Worms, and Wonder: A Guide for Creatively Integrating Gardening and Outdoor Learning Into Children's Lives,* by Kelly Johnson
- *12 Month Art And Nature Journal: Mindfully Color, Sketch. & Relax Your Way Into Nature*, by Kelly Johnson
- *Pressed: An Herbarium Inspired Art Journal*, by Kelly Johnson

Website & Blog

- The Wings, Worms, and Wonder: Creatively connecting humans and nature: *www.wingswormsandwonder.com/*
- Wonder Wednesday Activities, Ideas, and Information for fostering art and nature connection experiences: *wingswormsandwonder.com/blog/*
- Explore topics to supplement the information in this book including: Make your own Natural Insect repellent; How to Pack a Field Bag; To Pick or Not to Pick, a mini blog course in harvesting Part 1, Part 2, & Part 3; Mud Mania; & American Montessori Society Webinar & Montessori Foundation webcasts

Online Learning

Join the Wings, Worms, and Wonder online nature journaling school: *wings-worms-and-wonder-classroom.teachable.com*. Take classes at your own pace from your computer including: Let's Build a Garden eCourseUsing Nature Journal Prompts (Including a printable set of the Wings, Worms, and Wonder Nature Journal prompt cards)

Home & School Garden Building, Integration, and Outdoor Learning Consultations: *www.wingswormsandwonder.com/work-with-me/*

Books for Adults on Connecting Children and Nature

- *Sense of Wonder,* by Rachel Carson
- *Wild Play: Parenting Adventures in the Great Outdoors*, by David Sobel
- *In Defense of Childhood: Protecting Kids' Inner Wildness,* by Chris Mercogliano
- *The Great Outdoors: Restoring Children's Right to Play Outside,* by Mary S. Rivkin
- *Hollyhocks and Honeybees: Garden Projects for Young Children,* by Sara Starbuck, Marla Olthof, and Karen Midden
- *The Nature Fix: Why Nature Makes Us Happier, Healthier, and More Creative;* by Florence Williams
- *Last Child in the Woods: Saving Our Children From Nature-Deficit Disorder,* by Richard Louv
- *Listening to Nature: How to Deepen Your Awareness of Nature,* by Joseph Cornell
- *The Handbook of Nature Study,* by Anna Botsford Comstock
- *Whatever the Weather: Science Experiments and Art Activities that Explore the Wonders of Weather,* by Annie Richman and Dawn Suzette Smith

Books for Adults on Gardening

- *Trowel and Error: Over 700 Organic Remedies, Shortcuts, and Tips for the Gardener,* by Sharon Lovejoy
- *Mini Farming: How to Create a Sustainable Organic Garden in Your Backyard You Can Be Proud Of,* by Better Gardening Guides
- *Urban Gardening: How To Grow Food In Any City Apartment Or Yard No Matter How Small,* by Will Cook
- *Rodale's Basic Organic Gardening: A Beginner's Guide to Starting a Healthy Garden,* by Deborah L. Martin
- *Gardening for Butterflies: How You Can Attract and Protect Beautiful, Beneficial Insects,* by Xerces Society
- *Gardening for Animals: A Beginners Guide to Creating a Butterfly Garden and Wildlife Habitat,* by Popp Butterfly Conservatory
- *Bringing Nature Home: How You Can Sustain Wildlife with Native Plants,* by Douglas W. Tallamy
- *Beatrix Potter's Gardening Life: The plants and places that inspired the classic children's tales,* by Marta McDowell

Books for Adults on Montessori Early Childhood Development and Learning

- *How to Raise an Amazing Child The Montessori Way: A parent's guide to building creativity, confidence, and independence,* by Tim Seldin
- *Montessori From the Start: The Child at Home, from Birth to Age Three,* by Paula Lillard & Lynn Lillard Jessen
- *The Joyful Child: Montessori Global Wisdom for Birth to Three,* by Susan M. Stephenson
- *The World of the Child,* by Aline Wolf

Online Supply Resources

- Nature-Watch: *nature-watch.com*

    Educational nature products and craft activity kits designed to teach children about nature

- Montessori Services: *montessoriservices.com*

    Unique and specialized items, materials, and complementary resources. (Small pitchers, trays, nut crackers, natural blocks, books, tongs, baskets, and more)

- Fill Your Own Tea Bags: *naturalteabags.com/*

- Nut Milk Strainer bags: *rawnutmilkbag.com/*

- Community Playthings: *communityplaythings.com/products/outdoor*

    Natural hand crafted outdoor play furniture and wooden outdoor toys

Blogs & Online Resources

- Garden Climate Zone Information and Finder: *garden.org/nga/zipzone/*

- Nature Journaling: There are many sources online for free downloadable nature journals, or simply use plain paper: *vault.sierraclub.org/education/nature_journal.asp*

- Building Literacy: Nature Journals for Beginning Writers: *childhood101.com/nature-journals-for-beginning-writers/*

- Fostering Independence: Education Optimist: *educationoptimist.com/blog/how-to-help-them-do-it-for-themselves*

Blogs & Online Resources, con't.

- Build an Art Easel for Indoors and Out- Foster your child's inner creativity by building an easel with them: *thisoldhouse.com/how-to/how-to-build-easel*

- Music, Songs, and Finger Play-

    Magical Movement Company, Montessori Music and Arts: *magicalmovementcompany.com/for-kids*

- Nature Song resources- *songsforteaching.com/themeunits/circletimetheme.htm preschooleducation.com/scirclesong.shtml*

- Mud Day- Mud Mania: *wingswormsandwonder.com/wonder-wednesday-22-mud-mania/*

- Wilder Child- Resources and online Wildschooling community: *wilderchild.com/category/wild-activities/*

- Phonetic Planet- Nature Inspired early Childhood Literacy: *phoneticplanet.org/read*

- Trillium Montessori- Educational Printables, information, and inspiration: *trilliummontessori.org/resources-for-parents/*

- Age of Montessori- Nature at home and school: *ageofmontessori.org/montessori-for-parents-and-for-teachers/nature/*

- Natural Beach Living- Botany Activities: *naturalbeachliving.com/montessori-inspired-botany-kids/*

- Carrots Are Orange- Outdoor learning Resources: *carrotsareorange.com/outdoor-learning-resources/*

Blogs & Online Resources, con't.

- Teaching from a Tackle Box- Gardening: *teachingfromatacklebox.blogspot.com/2017/03/gardening-montessori-way.html*
- The Montessori Family Blog- Benefits and Activities for working on Vertical Surfaces: *themontessorifamily.com/why-your-child-should-work-on-a-vertical-surface-and-15-activities-to-try/*
- The Prepared Environment- Outdoor Play: *thepreparedenvironment.com/blog/playing-outside-is-more-than-just-fun-its-vital*
- Making Montessori Ours- Botany activities and pdf printables: *makingmontessoriours.com/search/label/Botany*
- Sharing Nature- Holistic ideas and activities by Joseph Cornell: *sharingnature.com/nature-activities.html*

Children's Nature Books

- *The Tales* series, by Beatrix Potter
- *The Flower Fairies* series, by Cicely Mary Barker
- *Ten Little Gumnuts*, by May Gibbs
- *Lola Plants a Garden*, by Anna McQuinn
- *We're Going on a Leaf Hunt*, by Steve Metzger
- *All the World*, by Liz Garton Scanlon
- *Baby's First Book of Birds and Colors*, by Phyllis Limbacher Tildes
- *Hello World! Backyard Bugs*, by Jill McDonald
- *My First Bird Book*, by Sharon Lovejoy

Children's Nature Books, con't.

- *Some Bugs*, by Angela DiTerlizzi
- *The Little Gardener* (Teenie Greenies series), by Jan Gerardi
- *Butterfly Counting and Colors*, by Jerry Pallotta
- *My Very First Book of Animal Homes*, by Eric Carle
- *Anywhere Farm*, by Phyllis Root
- *City Green*, by DyAnne DiSalvo Ryan
- *Little Seeds*, by Charles Ghigna
- *Compost Stew*, by Mary McKenna Siddals
- *Miss Maple's Seeds*, by Eliza Wheeler
- *Florette*, by Anna Walker
- *Sofia's Dream*, by Land Wilson
- *How to Grow a Friend*, by Sara Gillingham
- *Have Your Heard the Nesting Bird?*, by Rita Gray
- *On the Wing*, by David Elliot
- *Little Owl* series, by Divya Srinivasam
- *I am an Artist*, by Pat Lowery Collins
- *Inch by Inch: The garden song*, by David Mallett
- *Changes: A child's first poetry collection*, by Charlotte Zolotow
- *The Dandelion Seed*, by Joseph Anthony
- *The Story of the Root Children*, by Sibylle von Olfers

Children's Nature Books, con't.

- *Blueberries for Sal*, by Robert McCloskey
- *In the Trees, Honeybees*, by Lori Mortensen
- *The Snowy Day*, Ezra Jack Keats
- *Garden Toes*, by Peggy Nolan
- *Owl Moon*, by Jane Yolen
- *Animal Hide and Seek*, by Dahlov Ipcar
- *The Sun Egg*, by Elsa Beskow
- *The Curious Garden*, Peter Brown
- *Miss Rumphius*, Barbara Cooney
- By Emily Winfield Martin:

  The Littlest Family's Big Day, Day Dreamers, Dream Animals, Oddfellow's Orphanage

- By Kate Messner :
- *Over and Under the Snow, Up in the Garden and Down in the Dirt, Over and Under the Pond*
- by IKids publishing:
- *Little Helpers; The Five Senses; Little Seeds; In the Garden*
- By Gail Gibbons:
- *Monarch Butterfly; The Honey Makers; Spiders; Frogs; The Reasons for the seasons; Ladybugs; From Seed to Plant*
- By Lois Ehlert:
- *Growing Vegetable Soup; Planting a Rainbow; Eating the Alphabet; Red Leaf, Yellow Leaf; Feathers for Lunch; Nuts to You!; Hands; Waiting for Wings; Leaf Man*

"Once you learn to read, you will be forever free."

~Frederick Douglass

This children's book list is just the tip of the iceberg! I adore children's books and could go on for days, but this list is a starting point.

Embrace the learning power of beautiful illustrations. The text of an illustrated story or poem meant for older children can always be simplified or abbreviated for reading to younger children. I do this all the time.

Children's Herb Primer

These herbs are all child-safe, edible, and child-tested and approved. They offer many different colors, smells, tastes, and textures, making them great starter herbs for a children's sensory-based herb garden, potted or in-ground. Those that aren't suitable for your climate and growing zone can be bought as spices, added to play clay, and explored in kitchen play.

- **Mints** – Mints are wonderfully scented and available in many varieties from chocolate to pineapple to peppermint. Mints are a great herbal introduction and VERY easy to grow! Parts Used: leaves.
- **Stevia** – Recently, stevia's become a popular substitute for artificial sweeteners. This herb's leaves literally taste as if they are made of sugar. Parts Used: leaves and flowers.
- **Basil** – Basil is a classic culinary herb that also makes a delicious tea. (It doesn't taste like spaghetti!) Basil comes in many varieties beyond the classic, such as the purple-leaved Thai basil and lemon basil. Parts Used: leaves and flowers.
- **Bee Balm** – This flowering herb smells wonderful, makes a fragrant tea, and the pink flowers can be eaten fresh, too. Parts Used: leaves and flowers.
- **Lavender** – A classic favorite scent for bath and body care, the flowers also can be eaten in teas, breads, and desserts, and it tastes great with chocolate! Parts Used: leaves and flowers.
- **Fennel** – Fennel is a large feathery plant with a highly fragrant licorice flavor. The flowers are beautiful in cut arrangements, and it is a host plant for swallowtail butterflies. Parts Used: leaves, stalks, and bulbs.
- **Lemon verbena** – Euphorically scented, this shrubby herb is a must for uplifting scents, and it makes a delicious tea. Parts Used: leaves and flowers.
- **Shiso** – Sometimes called perilla or Japanese basil, this herb is great for cooking projects when studying Asia (especially in making sushi). Plant the purple-leaf variety to add dynamic color to the herb garden. Parts Used: leaves.
- **Nasturtium** – This herb has peppery-flavored leaves that introduces the children to a little spice without being spicy. Eat the bright flowers too. Parts Used: leaves and flowers.
- **Rosemary** – A popular culinary herb, rosemary is an easy-to-grow child-size shrub that likes to be ignored and left somewhat dry, and it offers a refreshing scent. Add rosemary to cooking projects, teas, or add sprigs to flower arrangements. Parts Used: leaves.

- **Aloe** – Famous for relieving sunburned skin, aloe has mild spikes on the leaves and is great for illustrating "prickly" in a safe way to young children. When cut, it produces a sticky gel. Parts Used: leaves, the gel is edible, but tastes VERY bitter.
- **Fenugreek** – This herb smells and tastes just like maple flavor and makes seed pods that rattle. Parts Used: seeds.
- **Chamomile** – Soothing and mild, this is a favorite tea of children. Parts Used: leaves and flowers.
- **Echinacea** – This herb is native to North America and makes gorgeous purple flowers that turn into very interesting seed pod heads. Parts Used: leaves in tea, flowers in arrangements, seed pods to explore through touch. (This tea is considered medicinal, so I don't recommend making echinacea tea in schools. Grow echinacea in the school garden for its beauty and ability to attract pollinators.)
- **Mullein** – Mullein is known as lamb's ear because its leaves are so soft and fuzzy. Once you pet the leaves you won't want to stop, but they also can be used in tea if you can resist petting them! When making mullein tea, be sure to strain these leaves through muslin to prevent any of the hairs from getting in the tea. They are soft on the leaf, but prickly on the throat. Parts Used: leaves.

- **Sorrel** – Sorrel is known to tea lovers by the name "Red Zinger," and is very popular in Central America and the Caribbean. This tart cousin of the hibiscus is beautiful at every stage of growth, and makes a tea children love! Parts Used: The "hips" (calyxes), flowers, leaves.

THE SCOOP

Offer the children a leaf of mint to eat with a leaf of stevia.

Surprise! It tastes like chewing gum – "Garden Gum!"

Works Cited

Carson, Rachel. *The Sense of Wonder.* New York: Harper & Row, text 1956, photos 1965. Print.

Checkley, Kathy. "The First Seven...and the Eight." *Educational Leadership* 55.1 (1997): 8. Print.

Hyun, Eunsook. "Ecological Human Brain and Young Children's 'Naturalist Intelligence' from the perspective of Developmentally and Culturally Appropriate Practice (DCAP)." *Presented at the Annual Conference of the American Educational Research Association.* 24-28 April 2000, New Orleans, LA, Annual Conference of the American Educational Research Association. Print.

---. "How Is Young Children's Intellectual Culture of Understanding Nature Different from Adults?" *Annual Meeting of the American Educational Research Association* 24-28 April 2000, New Orleans, LA, Annual Meeting of the American Educational Research Association. Print.

Kahn, Peter H., Jr and Stephen R. Kellert, eds. *Children and Nature: Psychological, Sociocultural, and Evolutionary Investigations.* Cambridge: MIT Press, 2002. Print.

Lillard, Paula Polk. *Montessori from the Start: The Child at Home, From Birth to Age Three.* New York: Schocken, 2003. Print.

Montessori, Maria. *The Discovery of the Child.* Chennai: Kalakshetra, 2006. Print.

--- *The Absorbent Mind.* Madras: Theosophical Publishing House. 1949. *Internet archive.org.* Web. 26 Nov. 2010.

---. "Montessori Talks to Parents I: Set the Children Free." *North American Montessori Teachers' Association The Child in Nature,* 2.2 (c.1990): 2. Print.

Plotkin, Bill. *Nature and the Human Soul: Cultivating Wholeness and Community in a Fragmented World.* Novato, CA: New World Library, 2008. Print.

Rivkin, Mary S. *The Great Outdoors: Restoring Children's Right to Play Outside.* Washington D.C.: National Association for the Education of Young Children. 1995. Print.

Wilson, Edward O. *Biophilia: The Human Bond with Other Species.* Cambridge: Harvard UP, 1984. Print.

About the Author

Kelly Johnson (BFA, AMS 6-9, MA) is an artist, author, Montessorian, nature journaling guide, and children's garden educator dividing her time between Neptune Beach, Florida, and Virginia's Blue Ridge Mountains.

She believes everyone can draw and that every one has a green thumb — they just need to be set up for success. When she isn't helping to creatively connect humans with the natural world, you'll find her with her sidekick Sean surfing, snowboarding, stargazing, and traveling the world in search of new wonders.

A graduate of Goddard College, the Savannah College of Art and Design, and the Florida Institute of Montessori Studies, Kelly shares her love of nature through her books, articles, blog, illustrations, workshops, international conference presentations, consultations, and courses — all created within her socially and environmentally responsible little company
Wings, Worms, and Wonder.

www.ingramcontent.com/pod-product-compliance
Lightning Source LLC
Chambersburg PA
CBHW041531220426
43672CB00002B/5